Pat Sajak's
MIXED-UP MADNESS

TRIUMPH
BOOKS

This book is available in quantity at special discounts for your group or organization. For further information, contact:

Triumph Books LLC
814 North Franklin Street
Chicago, Illinois 60610

Printed in U.S.A.
ISBN: 978-1-57243-986-3

Design by David L. Hoyt
Production by Patricia Frey

Pat Sajak's
CODE LETTER
MIXED-UP
MADNESS
AND MORE

CONTENTS

INSTRUCTIONS ···················· Page 2

PUZZLES ······················ Page 4

BONUS PUZZLES ················ Page 158

ANSWER KEY ··················· Page 181

PAT SAJAK's CODE LETTERS™ AND CODE NUMBERS™ INSTRUCTIONS

Using his new Code Letters and Code Numbers puzzle-play systems, Pat has created an all-new puzzle-solving experience. Certain letters or numbers in each puzzle get Coded with a symbol. If you can figure out a Code Letter or Code Number then you can fill in that letter or number throughout the puzzle on corresponding Coded spaces.

CODE LETTER™ SCRAMBLE EXAMPLE

CODE LETTER SCRAMBLE 6-LETTER WORDS

Use the Code Letters to help you unscramble the mixed-up letters to spell common words.

RIFMNO
#1 I N F O R M

WRTNHO
#5 ☐ ☐ ☐ O ☐ ☐

BELIRM
#2 ☐ I M ☐ ☐

GMDAEA
#6 ☐ ☐ M ☐ ☐ ☐

TINONO
#3 ☐ O ☐ I O

CIPSBE
#7 ☐ I ☐ ☐ ☆ ☐

AOPTOT
#4 ☆ O ☐ ☐ O

MECAAR
#8 ☐ ☐ M ☐ ☐ ☐

In the example scramble puzzle above:

All the △ Code Symbols = M
All the ◇ Code Symbols = O
All the □ Code Symbols = I

The Code Letters above apply to this example puzzle only. Other puzzles will have different Codes. You have to figure them out. When you do, you can fill them in throughout the puzzle.

2

CODE LETTER™ CROSSWORD EXAMPLE

If you fill in a space that has a Code Symbol (star, diamond, etc.), you can fill in that letter on all the other spaces with that Code Symbol.

In the example crossword puzzle:
All the ☆ Code Symbols = T
All the ◇ Code Symbols = R
All the □ Code Symbols = N
All the △ Code Symbols = E

CODE NUMBER™ SUDOKU EXAMPLE

Code Numbers work just like Code Letters, but for numbers.

In the example sudoku puzzle:
All the ☆ Code Symbols = 1
All the ♡ Code Symbols = 3

9	2	6	8	1	7	5	3♡	4
7	1☆	3♡	4	6	5	2	9	8
4	5	8	3	9	2	6	7	1☆
6	3♡	5	9	2	8	4	1	7
8	9	2	7	4	1☆	3♡	6	5
1☆	7	4	5	3	6	9	8	2
5	8	9	6	7	4	1☆	2	3♡
2	6	7	1	5	3♡	8	4	9
3	4	1	2	8	9	7	5	6

Pat Sajak's Code Letters and Code Numbers work with more than just scrambles, crosswords and sudoku puzzles. Regardless of the puzzle or game format, the same basic rules for filling in answers will apply.

CODE LETTER SCRAMBLE 5-LETTER WORDS

Unscramble the mixed-up letters to spell common words. Complete Code Letters instructions on pages 2 and 3.

OAELN
#1

AANSU
#2

NUINO
#3

NOCAB
#4

DOHNU
#5

LASHS
#6

LOEYD
#7

AORCG
#8

LTANP
#9

Pat Sajak's MIXED-UP MADNESS #2

CODE LETTER SCRAMBLE 5-LETTER WORDS

Unscramble the mixed-up letters to spell common words. Complete Code Letters instructions on pages 2 and 3.

#1 OSOPC

#2 OEHLW

#3 MTROU

#4 RLBTU

#5 LODUA

#6 ACLLO

#7 RPHOC

#8 DOWUL

#9 RIPCM

HOW DO YOU RANK?

0 - 1 completely filled in = F   6 completely filled in = B
2 - 3 completely filled in = D   7 completely filled in = B+
4 completely filled in = C   8 completely filled in = A
5 completely filled in = C+   9 completely filled in = A+

Pat Sajak's MIXED-UP MADNESS   #3

CODE LETTER LADDER

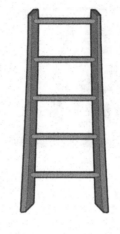

Unscramble the mixed-up letters to spell common words. Complete Code Letters instructions on pages 2 and 3.

PGURO

#1

TKECOP

#2

UDHETIO

#3

RDWRAAEH

#4

EOLSURNWF

#5

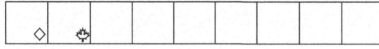

TSBALHEPIT

#6

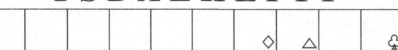

RTNAOTIOCNP

6 **#7**

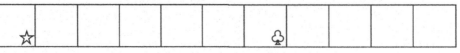

CODE LETTER LADDER

Unscramble the mixed-up letters to spell common words. Complete Code Letters instructions on pages 2 and 3.

U R I T F

#1

E M R O E V

#2

P U C E K C H

#3

D L I L A L N F

#4

N E S Y O R U T G

#5

K E I C O P C T K P

#6

N F S I C A I T G I N

#7

Pat Sajak's MIXED-UP MADNESS

#5

MOVIES

Unscramble the mixed-up letters to spell movie titles, as suggested by the out or order clues. Complete Code Letters instructions on pages 2 and 3.

FSCEACAR

#1

HIDAEDR

#2

NPUCIPITOFL

#3

HDTEHEFTORGA

#4

CATTNOC

#5

8

Continued on next page.

Pat Sajak's MIXED-UP MADNESS

GIVEORT

#6

STTHIGEN

#7

TPOTNA

#8

OUT OF ORDER CLUES
Assign each answer from the puzzle to a clue below (by writing "#1," "#2," etc.).

_____ 1994 movie directed by Quentin Tarantino

_____ 1994 Jodie Foster movie

_____ 1973 movie starring Robert Redford and Paul Newman

_____ 1988 Bruce Willis movie directed by John McTiernan

_____ 1970 movie starring George C. Scott

_____ 1972 "Best Picture" Oscar winner

_____ 1983 movie directed by Brian De Palma

_____ 1958 movie directed by Alfred Hitchcock

HOW DO YOU RANK?
0 - 1 completely filled in = F
2 - 3 completely filled in = D
4 - 5 completely filled in = C
6 completely filled in = B
7 completely filled in = A
8 completely filled in = A+

CODE LETTER LAUGHS: RIDDLES

What do you call a snowman vacationing in the Bahamas?

DALPEUD

| A | | P | U | D | D | L | E |

Unscramble the mixed-up letters to spell the answers to the riddles. Complete Code Letters instructions on pages 2 and 3.

RIDDLE: What goes up and down but doesn't move?

T R A S A I S E C A

#1 | | | | | | ♣ | | ☆ | | |

RIDDLE: What has four legs and a back but no body?

A C I A H R

#2 | | | | ☆ | | | ♣ | |

RIDDLE: What turns everything around but doesn't move?

R M R I R O A

#3 | | | | △ | ♣ | | | | |

Continued on next page.

Pat Sajak's MIXED-UP MADNESS

RIDDLE: What people travel the most?

A N R O S M

#4

RIDDLE: Who never gets his hair wet in the shower?

M A D N L A B A

#5

RIDDLE: What belongs to you, but is used more by others?

A R Y E O M U N

#6

RIDDLE: What piece of wood is like a king?

E L A U R R

#7

HOW DO YOU RANK?	0 - 1 completely filled in = F	5 completely filled in = B+
	2 completely filled in = D	6 completely filled in = A
	3 completely filled in = C	7 completely filled in = A+
	4 completely filled in = B	

ADJECTIVES

Unscramble the mixed-up letters to spell adjectives, as suggested by the out of order clues. Complete Code Letters instructions on pages 2 and 3.

BRIGHT SUNNY WARM

#1   YINSO

#2   KYICTR

#3   RYNEOR

#4   NTGOSR

#5   UIOIVSC

#6   TDITSAN

#7   CIESLPA

Continued on next page.

#8   E S U D I O V

#9   G H Y L T E N

#10 U J L E S A O

OUT OF ORDER CLUES
Assign each answer from the puzzle to a clue below (by writing "#1," "#2," etc.).

_____ A word that could be used to describe a movie that runs for more than three hours

_____ A word that can be used to describe a weightlifter who can bench 300 lbs.

_____ A word that can be used to describe someone who's mad that they don't have a new car like his or her neighbor

_____ A word that can be used to describe a group of children playing and screaming

_____ A word that can be used to describe a crook who's planning to con you out of your money

_____ A word that can be used to describe what walking across a tightrope is

_____ A word that can be used to describe something that's unique and important

_____ A word that can be used to describe an attacking wild animal

_____ A word that can be used to describe a grumpy, stubborn person

_____ A word that can be used to describe Pluto's location in relation to your location

HOW DO YOU RANK?
0 - 1 completely filled in = F
2 - 3 completely filled in = D
4 - 5 completely filled in = C
6 completely filled in = B
7 completely filled in = B+
8 completely filled in = A-
9 completely filled in = A
10 completely filled in = A+

13

MATH

$$2 \times 2 = 4$$
$$6 + 4 = 10$$
$$7 - 6 = 1$$
$$10 \times 2 = 20$$

Unscramble the mixed-up letters to spell out correct mathematical equations that fit into the answer boxes. Complete Code Letters instructions on pages 2 and 3.

FOR EXAMPLE:

NONTEOEOW

| O | N | E | | + | | O | N | E | | = | | T | W | O |

OTOSIFXUWR

#1 [   ][   ][   ] – [   ][   ][   ][△] = [   ][◇]

ZZROEROEZROE

#2 [   ][   ][△] × [   ][   ][△] = [   ][   ][△]

WEISRTETXOH

#3 [   ][   ][   ] ÷ [   ][◇] = [   ][♣][△][   ]

NTHEOIGNEIEN

#4 [   ][   ][   ] + [   ][   ][   ][♣] = [   ][   ][   ][   ]

14

Continued on next page.

Pat Sajak's MIXED-UP MADNESS

EFTFEIFIYVTN

#5 ☐☐☐ × ☐☐☐☐☐ = ☐☐☐☐☐(☆)

OEEOZRGZITHER

#6 ☐☐☐☐(♣)☐ × ☐☐☐(△)☐ = ☐☐☐(△)

EIYFNFOYTFTIF

#7 ☐☐☐☐☐(☆) × ☐☐☐ = ☐☐☐☐(☆)

ETRHINHETENERE

#8 ☐☐☐☐ ÷ ☐(♣)(△)☐ = ☐(♣)(△)☐

VEEVENTLEWLOEEN

#9 ☐☐☐ + ☐☐☐☐☐☐ = ☐☐(◇)☐☐☐

TEETNYWTTIYHNRT

#10 ☐(◇)☐☐☐(☆) + ☐☐☐ = ☐(♣)☐(△)☐(☆)

HOW DO YOU RANK?
0 - 1 completely filled in = F   7 completely filled in = B+
2 - 3 completely filled in = D-   8 completely filled in = A-
4 - 5 completely filled in = C   10 completely filled in = A+
6 completely filled in = B

15

ACTORS AND ACTRESSES

Unscramble the mixed-up letters to spell names of
actors and actresses, as suggested by the out or
order clues. Complete Code Letters instructions
on pages 2 and 3.

MLTIAENL

#1

LDSLIELYAF

#2

YNLARAINELU

#3

RGIASISENY

#4

MEIROEMOD

#5

Continued on next page.

Pat Sajak's MIXED-UP MADNESS

TNMAADOTM

#6 ☆ ☆ ♡ 🍁

ZRJFIEOLNPEEN

#7 🍁 🍁 ♡

NOEKVICANB

#8 🍁 ♡ 🍁

OUT OF ORDER CLUES
Assign each answer from the puzzle to a clue below (by writing "#1," "#2," etc.).

_____ Actress who played Truman Burbank's wife in "The Truman Show"

_____ Star of "G.I. Jane"

_____ Actor born in Massachusetts in 1970

_____ Actor who voiced Buzz Lightyear in "Toy Story"

_____ Actress who played Charlie in "Monster-in-Law"

_____ Actress who played Forrest Gump's mother

_____ Kyra Sedgwick's husband

_____ Actor who plays Det. Mac Taylor on TV

HOW DO YOU RANK?
0 - 1 completely filled in = F
2 - 3 completely filled in = D
4 - 5 completely filled in = C
6 completely filled in = B
7 completely filled in = A
8 completely filled in = A+

RHYMES WITH...

GO --- NO
TON --- FUN
BACK --- STACK
STUCK --- TRUCK
MISTER --- SISTER
SCANDAL --- SANDAL

Unscramble the mixed-up letters to spell common words, as suggested by the out of order clues. Complete Code Letters instructions on pages 2 and 3.

MIXED-UP ANSWER	ANSWER
#1 R T I D H	
#2 L G J N E U	
#3 U T B R T E	
#4 M U I S T M	
#5 S I P V E S A	
#6 Y L O R T Y A	
#7 R T R O E B H	

Continued on next page.

Pat Sajak's MIXED-UP MADNESS

#8 L E H W Y A T

#9 M R C E L B U

#10 H E C E L R F U

OUT OF ORDER CLUES
Assign each answer from the puzzle to a clue below (by writing "#1," "#2," etc.).

_____ Rhymes with PLUMMET

_____ Rhymes with HEALTHY

_____ Rhymes with TUMBLE

_____ Rhymes with TEARFUL

_____ Rhymes with STUTTER

_____ Rhymes with SMOTHER

_____ Rhymes with BUNGLE

_____ Rhymes with WORD

_____ Rhymes with LOYALTY

_____ Rhymes with MASSIVE

HOW DO YOU RANK?
0 - 1 completely filled in = F
2 - 3 completely filled in = D
4 - 5 completely filled in = C
6 completely filled in = B
7 completely filled in = B+
8 completely filled in = A-
9 completely filled in = A
10 completely filled in = A+

CODE LETTER LINK LADDER

Unscramble the mixed-up letters to spell names of actors/actresses and movies he or she starred in. Complete Code Letters instructions on pages 2 and 3.

Actors / Actresses

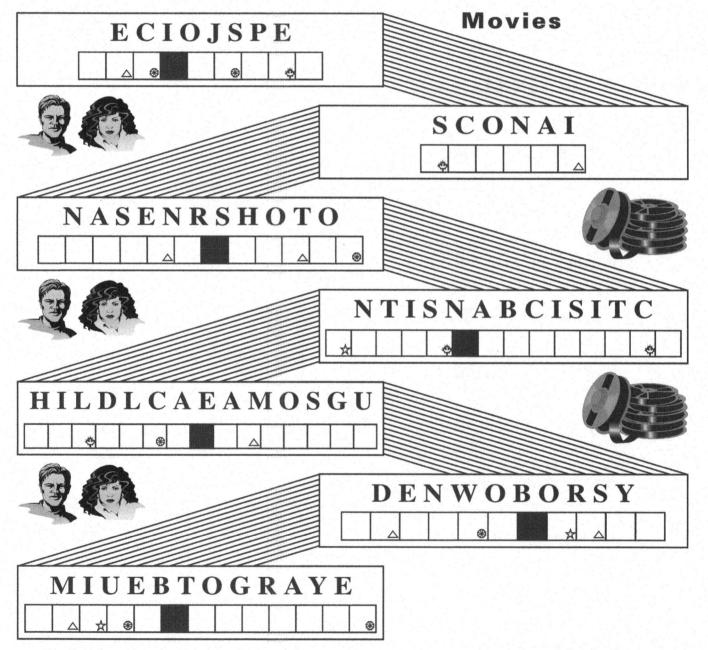

Movies

ECIOJSPE

SCONAI

NASENRSHOTO

NTISNABCISITC

HILDLCAEAMOSGU

DENWOBORSY

MIUEBTOGRAYE

Pat Sajak's MIXED-UP MADNESS

#12

CODE LETTER LINK LADDER

Unscramble the mixed-up letters to spell names of actors/actresses and movies he or she starred in. Complete Code Letters instructions on pages 2 and 3.

Actors / Actresses

Movies

EEFCBNFKAL

LPAABROHRER

LAECWDIBANL

ELACMI

EOCMIDLINNAK

HTARPEEAKCMEE

RGEOYCEGOLEON

21

TV SHOWS

Unscramble the mixed-up letters to spell TV show titles, as suggested by the out or order clues. Complete Code Letters instructions on pages 2 and 3.

YSDANYT
#1 ☆

NLESDIFE
#2 ☆

RRTATKES
#3 ♣

RTMTUENESHS
#4 △ ▢ ♡

VOSRVIRU
#5 ♡ ✳

Continued on next page.

Pat Sajak's **MIXED-UP MADNESS**

KNUMOEGS

#6

ROMAIECNIDLA

#7

SPTESRONAOSH

#8

OUT OF ORDER CLUES

Assign each answer from the puzzle to a clue below (by writing "#1," "#2," etc.).

_____ A CBS reality show

_____ A TV western that aired for almost 20 years

_____ Nighttime soap that premiered in 1981

_____ Show that aired o NBC from 1966 to 1969

_____ Very popular show that airs on Fox

_____ The #1 sitcom of the 1990s

_____ HBO crime drama

_____ Show featuring a house on Mockingbird Lane

HOW DO YOU RANK?

0 - 1 completely filled in = F
2 - 3 completely filled in = D
4 - 5 completely filled in = C
6 completely filled in = B
7 completely filled in = A
8 completely filled in = A+

Pat Sajak's MIXED-UP MADNESS #14

#14

CODE LETTER SCRAMBLE 5-LETTER WORDS

Unscramble the mixed-up letters to spell common words. Complete Code Letters instructions on pages 2 and 3.

ONNWK
#1

HAAPL
#2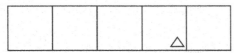

DECIM
#3

LATOT
#4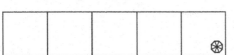

AWMAC
#5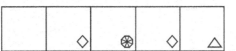

SOISA
#6

VNERA
#7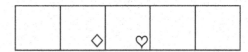

VAREB
#8

AHSOC
#9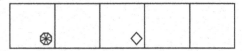

HOW DO YOU RANK?

0 - 1 completely filled in = F	6 completely filled in = B
2 - 3 completely filled in = D	7 completely filled in = B+
4 completely filled in = C	8 completely filled in = A
5 completely filled in = C+	9 completely filled in = A+

CODE LETTER SCRAMBLE 5-LETTER WORDS

Unscramble the mixed-up letters to spell common words. Complete Code Letters instructions on pages 2 and 3.

CIOEV
#1

NTEDR
#2

VIOEM
#3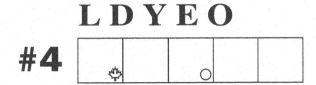

LDYEO
#4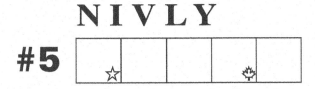

NIVLY
#5

BUSAC
#6

CHHTA
#7

LHOEL
#8

NBHCU
#9

25

CELEBRITY BIRTHDAYS

Unscramble the mixed-up letters to spell names of celebrities, as suggested by their birthdays. Complete Code Letters instructions on pages 2 and 3.

BIRTHDAY		CELEBRITY

#1 6-28-1948 — AYTAHKTEBS

#2 6-15-1963 — LEUTHNNEH

#3 4-18-1961 — EVESELNAEJ

#4 8-14-1945 — SETRNIMAVTE

#5 9-17-1948 — NHRIRETJOT

CELEBRITY BIRTHDAYS

Unscramble the mixed-up letters to spell names of celebrities, as suggested by their birthdays. Complete Code Letters instructions on pages 2 and 3.

BIRTHDAY   **CELEBRITY**

#1   3-10-1940

U R O I H C S N R C K

#2   3-20-1937

R E R Y E D E R J

#3   1-26-1925

U W P E N M N A L A

#4   8-23-1949

L N L H Y L O G E S E

#5   10-14-1927

M E R G O E O R O R

CODE LETTER LADDER

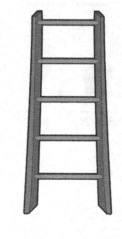

Unscramble the mixed-up letters to spell common words. Complete Code Letters instructions on pages 2 and 3.

RGMOO

#1

DMIELD

#2

BIEGERC

#3

EDOSLRHU

#4

THFIULRFG

#5

CNMEIEETXT

#6

NITPUCLIOBA

#7

28

Pat Sajak's MIXED-UP MADNESS #19

CODE LETTER LADDER

Unscramble the mixed-up letters to spell common words. Complete Code Letters instructions on pages 2 and 3.

COFKL

#1

XFREEL

#2

DRHOACR

#3

THCSUTEN

#4

KNMHAUIDN

#5

OPSUESINNS

#6

AMTSEIETLNN

#7

MOVIES

Unscramble the mixed-up letters to spell movie titles, as suggested by the out or order clues. Complete Code Letters instructions on pages 2 and 3.

RCJUPSRSIAKA

#1

BCFILUTHG

#2

CLBAANAASC

#3

ROUFVGINEN

#4

WDOREINWRA

#5

Continued on next page.

Pat Sajak's MIXED-UP MADNESS

SNWIEST

#6

EGAEDGJEDG

#7

VEBRAETARH

#8

OUT OF ORDER CLUES
Assign each answer from the puzzle to a clue below (by writing "#1," "#2," etc.).

_____ 1942 "Best Picture" Oscar winner

_____ 1954 movie in which Grace Kelly played Lisa Carol Fremont

_____ 1992 movie starring and directed by Clint Eastwood

_____ 1995 movie starring and directed by Mel Gibson

_____ 1993 movie based on a book by Michael Crichton

_____ 1985 Glenn Close movie

_____ 1999 movie starring Brad Pitt and Edward Norton

_____ 1985 Harrison Ford movie

HOW DO YOU RANK?
0 - 1 completely filled in = F
2 - 3 completely filled in = D
4 - 5 completely filled in = C
6 completely filled in = B
7 completely filled in = A
8 completely filled in = A+

CODE LETTER LAUGHS: RIDDLES

Unscramble the mixed-up letters to spell the answers to the riddles. Complete Code Letters instructions on pages 2 and 3.

What do you call a snowman vacationing in the Bahamas?

DALPEUD

| A | ■ | P | U | D | D | L | E |

RIDDLE: What fly has laryngitis?

F E A O Y S R L H

#1

| | ■ | △ | | | | ☆ | | □ |

RIDDLE: What is an ant dictator?

N R A T Y T A

#2

| | ■ | | □ | | | |

RIDDLE: What is the most valuable fish?

F D A O I S L H G

#3

| | ■ | | | | | ☆ | | △ |

Continued on next page.

RIDDLE: What wears shoes but has no feet?

A E S D A L K I W

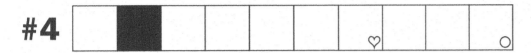

#4

RIDDLE: How did the clock feel when no one wound it up?

W N U O D N R

#5

RIDDLE: Where do sick steamships go?

K C T O E O T D H

#6

RIDDLE: How does a hot dog speak?

L K F N R Y A

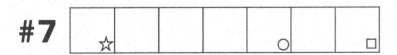

#7

HOW DO YOU RANK?	0 - 1 completely filled in = F	5 completely filled in = B+
	2 completely filled in = D	6 completely filled in = A
	3 completely filled in = C	7 completely filled in = A+
	4 completely filled in = B	

CODE LETTER SCRAMBLE 6-LETTER WORDS

Unscramble the mixed-up letters to spell common words. Complete Code Letters instructions on pages 2 and 3.

RAWYIA

#1

LETELP

#6

YNCIGR

#2

NSLOSE

#7

TLDNAE

#3

RIELFP

#8

ATOLPS

#4

NOIOMD

#9

TUDDEC

#5

HOW DO YOU RANK?

0 - 1 completely filled in = F   6 completely filled in = B
2 - 3 completely filled in = D   7 completely filled in = B+
4 completely filled in = C   8 completely filled in = A
5 completely filled in = C+   9 completely filled in = A+

CODE LETTER SCRAMBLE
6-LETTER WORDS

Unscramble the mixed-up letters to spell common words. Complete Code Letters instructions on pages 2 and 3.

E R R O C G

#1

N E E L K N

#6

A F G U L R

#2

D R C E U S

#7

B L R I E M

#3

T E D I L A

#8

D L B I E R

#4

R N O I M F

#9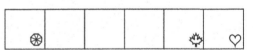

C E M B O E

#5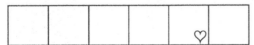

HOW DO YOU RANK?

0 - 1 completely filled in = F   6 completely filled in = B
2 - 3 completely filled in = D   7 completely filled in = B+
4 completely filled in = C   8 completely filled in = A
5 completely filled in = C+   9 completely filled in = A+

Pat Sajak's MIXED-UP MADNESS

ACTORS AND ACTRESSES

Unscramble the mixed-up letters to spell names of actors and actresses, as suggested by the out or order clues. Complete Code Letters instructions on pages 2 and 3.

SNMIBEOLG

#1

CTORIUEMS

#2

RFCASREIERIH

#3

MRROOEOEGR

#4

LWAEBCAINDL

#5

Continued on next page.

Pat Sajak's MIXED-UP MADNESS

NWJYOAENH

#6

SEGLNLOENC

#7

ORGEOECYLNEGO

#8

OUT OF ORDER CLUES
Assign each answer from the puzzle to a clue below (by writing "#1," "#2," etc.).

_____ Actor born in England in 1927

_____ Actor who played Jack Ryan in "The Hunt for Red October"

_____ Director and star of "Man Without a Face"

_____ Nephew of singer/actress Rosemary Clooney

_____ Actor whose real last name is Mapother

_____ "Star Wars" star born in 1956

_____ Actor who died in 1979 at age 72

_____ Actress who played Alex Forrest in "Fatal Attraction"

HOW DO YOU RANK?
0 - 1 completely filled in = F
2 - 3 completely filled in = D
4 - 5 completely filled in = C
6 completely filled in = B
7 completely filled in = A
8 completely filled in = A+

37

CODE LETTER LAUGHS: RIDDLES

Unscramble the mixed-up letters to spell the answers to the riddles. Complete Code Letters instructions on pages 2 and 3.

What do you call a snowman vacationing in the Bahamas?

DALPEUD

A	■	P	U	D	D	L	E

RIDDLE: What is bought by the yard and worn by the foot?

E C A R T A P

#1

	■					☆

RIDDLE: What is the healthiest kind of water?

L T W E L E A R W

#2

	🍁			■		🍁		☆	

RIDDLE: What is the perfect cure for dandruff?

N S D A B L E S

#3

	♣						

38

Continued on next page.

RIDDLE: What has a big mouth but doesn't say a word?

R R I E A V

#4

RIDDLE: What has a head, can't think, but drives?

M A A H R M E

#5

RIDDLE: What happens when you throw a green rock in the Red Sea?

W S I G T E T E T

#6

RIDDLE: What do you get if you cross an insect and a rabbit?

N S B U Y U B N G

#7

MATH

$2 \times 2 = 4$
$6 + 4 = 10$
$7 - 6 = 1$
$10 \times 2 = 20$

Unscramble the mixed-up letters to spell out correct mathematical equations that fit into the answer boxes. Complete Code Letters instructions on pages 2 and 3.

FOR EXAMPLE:

NONTEOEOW

$\boxed{O\,N\,E} + \boxed{O\,N\,E} = \boxed{T\,W\,O}$

NUFOFRUROOE

#1 $\boxed{\,\star} \div \boxed{} = \boxed{\,\star}$

FTORRNUEOEHE

#2 $\boxed{} + \boxed{\,\maltese\,} = \boxed{\,\star}$

RWFETEEVHTIO

#3 $\boxed{\,\square} - \boxed{} = \boxed{\,\maltese\,}$

RRZFOEORUFUO

#4 $\boxed{\,\star} + \boxed{\diamond\,} = \boxed{\,\star}$

Continued on next page.

Pat Sajak's MIXED-UP MADNESS

NVFTEOSVIEEW

#5 ☐☐☐☐☐ + ☐☐☐ = ☐☐☐☐☐

OZZRZREROOEE

#6 ☐☐☐☐☐ − ☐☐☐☐☐ = ☐☐☐☐

TOGFERHTIOWU

#7 ☐☐☐☐☐ ÷ ☐☐☐☐ = ☐☐☐

XTYRTWTOHISTIY

#8 ☐☐☐☐☐☐ ÷ ☐☐☐ = ☐☐☐☐☐

EOREESZEVNVSNE

#9 ☐☐☐☐☐ − ☐☐☐☐ = ☐☐☐☐☐

TEEIHRETENHENR

#10 ☐☐☐☐ × ☐☐☐☐ = ☐☐☐☐

TV SHOWS

Unscramble the mixed-up letters to spell TV show titles, as suggested by the out or order clues. Complete Code Letters instructions on pages 2 and 3.

CTPEOPLEAYN

#1

PSYDHPAYA

#2

ZNOAANB

#3

AUMDOTUYOAB

#4

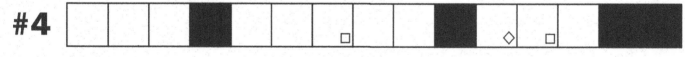

MFAYILIEST

#5

42

Continued on next page.

Pat Sajak's MIXED-UP MADNESS

SRFRIEA

#6 [grid with triangle marker in 2nd box]

DMFELYUIAF

#7 [grid with triangle, diamond, triangle markers]

HMTEISNSOSP

#8 [grid with star and square markers]

OUT OF ORDER CLUES
Assign each answer from the puzzle to a clue below (by writing "#1," "#2," etc.).

_____ TV western that aired on NBC that premiered in 1959

_____ Popular spinoff that premiered in 1993

_____ TV show based on a novel by Grace Metalious

_____ Popular game show hosted by one of the stars of "Hogan's Heroes"

_____ Sitcom that made it to #1 in the ratings

_____ Popular sitcom set in Columbus, Ohio

_____ Long-running animated show

_____ Sitcom that featured the Buchmans

CODE LETTER LADDER

Unscramble the mixed-up letters to spell common words. Complete Code Letters instructions on pages 2 and 3.

SPUYH

#1

BCANRH

#2

LBACNYO

#3

ABEORVIH

#4

DAPEPHENR

#5

SGETNRTHNE

#6

MNVEIROTNEN

#7

44

CODE LETTER LADDER

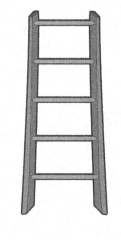

Unscramble the mixed-up letters to spell common words. Complete Code Letters instructions on pages 2 and 3.

XTOCI

#1

NREUNR

#2

TARTCTA

#3

SOLCOSLA

#4

CMIFAILSE

#5

PEMSRBMEIH

#6

RHACOPELIAG

#7

45

ACTORS AND ACTRESSES

Unscramble the mixed-up letters to spell names of actors and actresses, as suggested by the out of order clues. Complete Code Letters instructions on pages 2 and 3.

NVRDALYOEGN

#1

RAIERSDH

#2

LIMNCOIDANEK

#3

PTERYELREMS

#4

DKDAOYARYN

#5

Continued on next page.

Pat Sajak's MIXED-UP MADNESS

NMTVEATRIES

#6

RMEIDUEPHYD

#7

AHGLIEWOND

#8

OUT OF ORDER CLUES
Assign each answer from the puzzle to a clue below (by writing "#1," "#2," etc.).

_____ Actress born in Hawaii who played Virginia Woolf in "The Hours"

_____ Kate Hudson's mother

_____ Actor who played Det. Roger Murtaugh in "Lethal Weapon"

_____ Actor born in Waco, Texas in 1945

_____ Actor born in Brooklyn in 1961

_____ Actress who played Karen Silkwood in "Silkwood"

_____ Actor born in Canada who starred in "Spies Like Us"

_____ Actor who played Jackson Pollock in "Pollock"

HOW DO YOU RANK?
0 - 1 completely filled in = F
2 - 3 completely filled in = D
4 - 5 completely filled in = C
6 completely filled in = B
7 completely filled in = A
8 completely filled in = A+

47

CODE LETTER LINK LADDER

Unscramble the mixed-up letters to spell names of actors/actresses and the movies that "link" them. Complete Code Letters instructions on pages 2 and 3.

Actors / Actresses

Movies

LABYSLYTILRC

	△		□	□	■		♣				□

TSPROEAIGFR

		♣			■			♣	

REGEWRDBAIN

		△	♣		■		◇				♣

KAOWBCLDIW

	△	□			■		◇			◇

NIESPOEHNDPR

						■	✸				♣

SESROIHO

✸						♣	

NEKMGECAHAN

				■		✸				

48

CODE LETTER LINK LADDER

Unscramble the mixed-up letters to spell names of actors/actresses and the movies that "link" them. Complete Code Letters instructions on pages 2 and 3.

Actors / Actresses

Movies

TRKFESHEIWROAT

AIORCPNOM

DISFTJEOEOR

NTCOTAC

SEAOWSMJDO

NXNIO

EWBTEORPOSHO

49

CODE LETTER LAUGHS: RIDDLES

Unscramble the mixed-up letters to spell the answers to the riddles. Complete Code Letters instructions on pages 2 and 3.

What do you call a snowman vacationing in the Bahamas?

DALPEUD

A		P	U	D	D	L	E

RIDDLE: How should you treat a baby goat?

KALIDEIK

#1

RIDDLE: What kind of pliers do you use in arithmetic?

SIPMLLERIUT

#2

RIDDLE: On what kind of ships do students study?

PHSCSORAHISL

#3

Continued on next page.

RIDDLE: What kind of pool can't you swim in?

OCLAPOAR

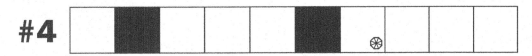

#4

RIDDLE: What is always coming but never arrives?

ROORTWMO

#5

RIDDLE: What has a foot on each end and one in the middle?

RCYDKATIAS

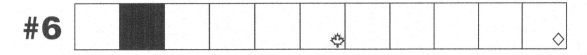

#6

RIDDLE: What is dark but made by light?

SAAODWH

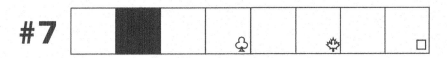

#7

HOW DO YOU RANK?

0 - 1 completely filled in = F
2 completely filled in = D
3 completely filled in = C
4 completely filled in = B
5 completely filled in = B+
6 completely filled in = A
7 completely filled in = A+

CELEBRITY BIRTHDAYS

Unscramble the mixed-up letters to spell names of celebrities, as suggested by their birthdays. Complete Code Letters instructions on pages 2 and 3.

BIRTHDAY	CELEBRITY
#1 3-16-1926	**R W S L J Y E I R E**
#2 9-25-1951	**A M R L A H L M K I**
#3 8-31-1949	**H E G E A C R R I D R**
#4 5-19-1950	**C J R S N E A G E O**
#5 9-9-1960	**H G R G N A T H U**

CELEBRITY BIRTHDAYS

Unscramble the mixed-up letters to spell names of celebrities, as suggested by their birthdays. Complete Code Letters instructions on pages 2 and 3.

BIRTHDAY	CELEBRITY

#1 3-15-1935

RIDUSHCHDJ

#2 3-19-1947

ENSLONGLEC

#3 1-21-1956

AIVSDNGAEE

#4 10-8-1939

ANHGAOUPL

#5 11-21-1945

LIHWOEDAGN

CODE LETTER LADDER

Unscramble the mixed-up letters to spell common words. Complete Code Letters instructions on pages 2 and 3.

LOHEL

#1

MUUTNA

#2

GCAAKPE

#3

COHEALES

#4

STEEXIENV

#5

UBSEOLDPNL

#6

RSTOREOEPHU

54 #7

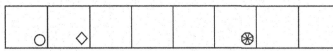

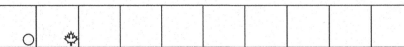
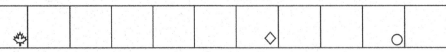

CODE LETTER LADDER

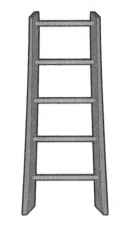

Unscramble the mixed-up letters to spell common words. Complete Code Letters instructions on pages 2 and 3.

N I J O T

#1

C R U S K U

#2

T S T I N O A

#3

N C O I R E L H

#4

A N S E U O R V P

#5

R S R E A T A N U T

#6

U B M H I N I R D M G

#7

CODE LETTER LAUGHS: RIDDLES

Unscramble the mixed-up letters to spell the answers to the riddles. Complete Code Letters instructions on pages 2 and 3.

What do you call a snowman vacationing in the Bahamas?

DALPEUD

| A | | P | U | D | D | L | E |

RIDDLE: What is the hottest part of a man's face?

N H I S B I E U S R S D

#1

RIDDLE: What kind of house weighs the least?

S H G L A I O H U E T

#2

RIDDLE: What branch of the army do babies join?

F R E Y T I A N N T H

#3

56

Continued on next page.

RIDDLE: What doesn't get any wetter no matter how much it rains?

A O T E E N H C

#4

RIDDLE: What horses keep late hours?

S E G M N I A R H T

#5

RIDDLE: What happened to the sardine when it didn't show up for work?

N W S I T A C N D E A

#6

RIDDLE: What kind of phone makes music?

A H N S O A P O E X

#7

HOW DO YOU RANK?	0 - 1 completely filled in = F	5 completely filled in = B+
	2 completely filled in = D	6 completely filled in = A
	3 completely filled in = C	7 completely filled in = A+
	4 completely filled in = B	

MOVIES

Unscramble the mixed-up letters to spell movie titles, as suggested by the out or order clues. Complete Code Letters instructions on pages 2 and 3.

SKCSLICIERYT

#1

ARSUMNPE

#2

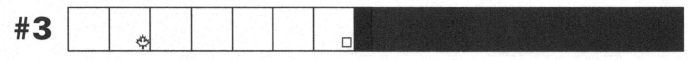

SDAAEUM

#3

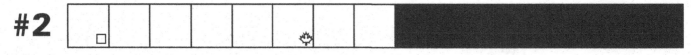

GEHTTINH

#4

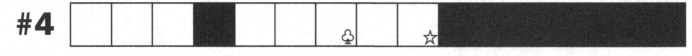

NOHINOHG

#5

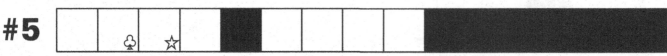

Continued on next page.

Pat Sajak's MIXED-UP MADNESS

XTMRATIEH

#6

XTRHCEOITSE

#7

GNNOKIKG

#8

OUT OF ORDER CLUES
Assign each answer from the puzzle to a clue below (by writing "#1," "#2," etc.).

_____ 1984 "Best Picture" Oscar winner

_____ 1982 movie starring Kurt Russell

_____ 1999 movie written and directed by the Wachowski brothers

_____ 1978 movie based on a comic book character

_____ 1973 horror movie

_____ 1991 movie starring Billy Crystal

_____ 1952 movie starring Gary Cooper

_____ 1933 movie starring Fay Ray

HOW DO YOU RANK?

0 - 1 completely filled in = F
2 - 3 completely filled in = D
4 - 5 completely filled in = C
6 completely filled in = B
7 completely filled in = A
8 completely filled in = A+

59

CODE LETTER SCRAMBLE
6-LETTER WORDS

Unscramble the mixed-up letters to spell common words. Complete Code Letters instructions on pages 2 and 3.

LIEPPM

#1

CMAOIT

#2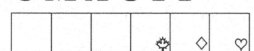

AIRINS

#3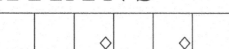

CELOTK

#4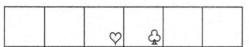

HNCOES

#5

TLTIOE

#6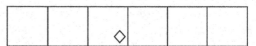

KAITEN

#7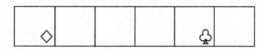

ONOHKU

#8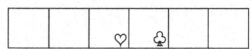

KEDCTO

#9

HOW DO YOU RANK?

0 - 1 completely filled in = F	6 completely filled in = B
2 - 3 completely filled in = D	7 completely filled in = B+
4 completely filled in = C	8 completely filled in = A
5 completely filled in = C+	9 completely filled in = A+

Pat Sajak's MIXED-UP MADNESS #41

CODE LETTER SCRAMBLE
6-LETTER WORDS

Unscramble the mixed-up letters to spell common words. Complete Code Letters instructions on pages 2 and 3.

#1 LREGIB

#2 DISENI

#3 CLIEPS

#4 MRBEOB

#5 TDNEEX

#6 MXHEEU

#7 CARKEB

#8 DKAEMR

#9 URLGFA

RHYMES WITH...

GO --- NO
TON --- FUN
BACK --- STACK
STUCK --- TRUCK
MISTER --- SISTER
SCANDAL --- SANDAL

Unscramble the mixed-up letters to spell common words, as suggested by the out of order clues. Complete Code Letters instructions on pages 2 and 3.

MIXED-UP ANSWER   **ANSWER**

#1 CAOLV

#2 ABRTBI

#3 LDEEDP

#4 SISNAHP

#5 RFUFEAL

#6 RSCTUDA

#7 PRECTMU

Continued on next page.

Pat Sajak's MIXED-UP MADNESS

#8 MRTMESA

#9 NTFIUANO

#10 GHDTUERA

OUT OF ORDER CLUES
Assign each answer from the puzzle to a clue below (by writing "#1," "#2," etc.).

_____ Rhymes with TRUMPET

_____ Rhymes with HAMMER

_____ Rhymes with TEARFUL

_____ Rhymes with WATER

_____ Rhymes with MUSTARD

_____ Rhymes with BANISH

_____ Rhymes with LOCAL

_____ Rhymes with MOUNTAIN

_____ Rhymes with MEDAL

_____ Rhymes with HABIT

HOW DO YOU RANK?
0 - 1 completely filled in = F
2 - 3 completely filled in = D
4 - 5 completely filled in = C
6 completely filled in = B
7 completely filled in = B+
8 completely filled in = A-
9 completely filled in = A
10 completely filled in = A+

ANIMALS

Unscramble the mixed-up letters to spell names of animals, as suggested by the out of order clues. Complete Code Letters instructions on pages 2 and 3.

#1 TPRAHEN

#2 UTKMARS

#3 AOCRCNO

#4 PLAEOENT

#5 EPNLETHA

#6 OKNARAOG

#7 DCROOIECL

Continued on next page.

Pat Sajak's MIXED-UP MADNESS

#8 **KNPCIMUH**

#9 **STMAOEMR**

#10 **UCIOPRNEP**

OUT OF ORDER CLUES

Assign each answer from the puzzle to a clue below (by writing "#1," "#2," etc.).

_____ Ruminant of the family Bovidae, chiefly of Africa and Asia

_____ Nocturnal carnivore with a sharp snout and a bushy, ringed tail

_____ Plant-eating marsupial

_____ Large tawny cat

_____ Large, aquatic, North American rodent

_____ Squirrellike, South and Central American monkey

_____ North American rodent known for its spines

_____ Powerful reptile

_____ Small, striped mammal

_____ Large pachyderm

HOW DO YOU RANK?

0 - 1 completely filled in = F
2 - 3 completely filled in = D
4 - 5 completely filled in = C
6 completely filled in = B
7 completely filled in = B+
8 completely filled in = A-
9 completely filled in = A
10 completely filled in = A+

Pat Sajak's MIXED-UP MADNESS #44

MATH

Unscramble the mixed-up letters to spell out correct mathematical equations that fit into the answer boxes. Complete Code Letters instructions on pages 2 and 3.

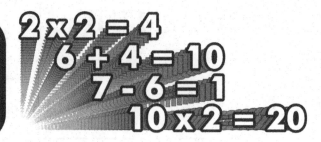

$$2 \times 2 = 4$$
$$6 + 4 = 10$$
$$7 - 6 = 1$$
$$10 \times 2 = 20$$

FOR EXAMPLE:

NONTEOEOW

ONE + ONE = TWO

HWTGNTEOIET

#1 ☐☐☐☐(△) + ☐☐(◇) = ☐☐☐

FWNEOTVTIE

#2 ☐☐☐☐ ÷ ☐☐☐(☆) = ☐☐(◇)

EEIORXOZSZR

#3 ☐☐☐(♡) × ☐☐☐☐☐ = ☐☐☐☐

LSTWXXEVIESI

#4 ☐☐☐(♡) + ☐☐☐(♡) = ☐☐(◇)☐☐(☆)

Continued on next page.

Pat Sajak's MIXED-UP MADNESS

ZERRIYEXZOTOS

#5 ☐☐☐♡☐ × ☐☐☐☐ = ☐☐☐☐

VNRVNELOESUEFEE

#6 ☐☐☐☆☐ + ☐☐☐☐ = ☐☐☐☆☐

NIERWLEVHETNEET

#7 ☐☐☐☐ + ☐☐△☐☐ = ☐☐◇☐☐☆☐

ELVETEEVWOENLNE

#8 ☐☐☐ + ☐☐☐☆☐ = ☐☐◇☐☐☆☐

EEIFNHETREIEVTFF

#9 ☐☐☐☐☐☐☐ ÷ ☐☐△☐☐ = ☐☐☆☐

HENOENEDUDRTNETN

#10 ☐☐☐ × ☐☐☐ = ☐☐☐   ☐△☐☐☐☐☐

HOW DO YOU RANK?	0 - 1 completely filled in = F	7 completely filled in = B+
	2 - 3 completely filled in = D-	8 completely filled in = A-
	4 - 5 completely filled in = C	10 completely filled in = A+
	6 completely filled in = B	

67

ACTORS AND ACTRESSES

Unscramble the mixed-up letters to spell names of actors and actresses, as suggested by the out or order clues. Complete Code Letters instructions on pages 2 and 3.

NSENANOEYCR

#1

EKTESINLTWA

#2

RYMIMESKE

#3

SNRSEEUOR

#4

NGTANEEEINNBT

#5

Continued on next page.

Pat Sajak's MIXED-UP MADNESS

RKINASIGEBM

#6

NOAFRENREMAMG

#7

SCINOLACEGA

#8

OUT OF ORDER CLUES

Assign each answer from the puzzle to a clue below (by writing "#1," "#2," etc.).

_____ "Saturday Night Live" star born in Canada in 1963

_____ Actress who played Dr. Molly Griswold in "Tin Cup"

_____ Actor born in Scotland in 1930

_____ Actress who played Vicki Vale in "Batman"

_____ Warren Beatty's wife

_____ Nephew of Francis Ford Coppola

_____ "Titanic" star born in England in 1975

_____ Actor who played God in "Bruce Almighty"

HOW DO YOU RANK?

0 - 1 completely filled in = F
2 - 3 completely filled in = D
4 - 5 completely filled in = C
6 completely filled in = B
7 completely filled in = A
8 completely filled in = A+

CODE LETTER LAUGHS: RIDDLES

Unscramble the mixed-up letters to spell the answers to the riddles. Complete Code Letters instructions on pages 2 and 3.

What do you call a snowman vacationing in the Bahamas?

DALPEUD

A		P	U	D	D	L	E

RIDDLE: What did Batman buy at the pet shop?

O B R I N A

#1

RIDDLE: What is another name for a telephone booth?

E B C X H R O T A A T

#2

RIDDLE: What food is good for the brain?

U D S N O E L O P O

#3

70

Continued on next page.

Pat Sajak's **MIXED-UP MADNESS**

RIDDLE: What does a wicked chicken lay?

S G E D E I D G L V E

#4

RIDDLE: What is a ghoul's favorite food?

A G O S U L H

#5

RIDDLE: What famous Greek might have invented baseball?

M E H O R

#6

RIDDLE: If fish lived on land, where would they live?

N I F N L I A D N

#7

HOW DO YOU RANK?	0 - 1 completely filled in = F	5 completely filled in = B+
	2 completely filled in = D	6 completely filled in = A
	3 completely filled in = C	7 completely filled in = A+
	4 completely filled in = B	

TV SHOWS

Unscramble the mixed-up letters to spell TV show titles, as suggested by the out or order clues. Complete Code Letters instructions on pages 2 and 3.

WSTEUPMETHOHP

#1

WOANTELRORDH

#2

HPCICOOEAGH

#3

BOOLUMC

#4

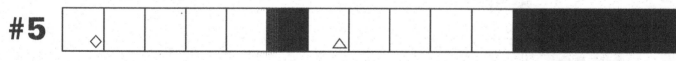

GTWNAOINAR

#5

Continued on next page.

Pat Sajak's MIXED-UP MADNESS

CEIOLUYLV

#6

NATNENYH

#7

CFTEFIOHE

#8

OUT OF ORDER CLUES
Assign each answer from the puzzle to a clue below (by writing "#1," "#2," etc.).

_____ Medical drama set in the Midwest

_____ Show that aired on NBC from 1957 to 1962 before moving to ABC

_____ TV police drama that shared its name with that of its lead character

_____ Show created by Jim Henson

_____ CBS sitcom that aired from 1993 to 1999

_____ Long-running soap opera

_____ NBC sitcom based in a British sitcom

_____ Sitcom that was #1 for three consecutive seasons

HOW DO YOU RANK?

0 - 1 completely filled in = F
2 - 3 completely filled in = D
4 - 5 completely filled in = C
6 completely filled in = B
7 completely filled in = A
8 completely filled in = A+

CODE LETTER SCRAMBLE 6-LETTER WORDS

Unscramble the mixed-up letters to spell common words. Complete Code Letters instructions on pages 2 and 3.

V L S I W E

#1

U K S N N E

#2

F I M F N U

#3

O N L A O S

#4

G H A R A N

#5

H G S E R U

#6

K A E T M R

#7

A K S E Y N

#8

K T I W C E

#9

HOW DO YOU RANK?

0 - 1 completely filled in = F
2 - 3 completely filled in = D
4 completely filled in = C
5 completely filled in = C+
6 completely filled in = B
7 completely filled in = B+
8 completely filled in = A
9 completely filled in = A+

Pat Sajak's MIXED-UP MADNESS #49

CODE LETTER SCRAMBLE
6-LETTER WORDS

Unscramble the mixed-up letters to spell common words. Complete Code Letters instructions on pages 2 and 3.

DSMEKA

#1

DUTISN

#2

TELCTU

#3

RIEGRD

#4

PLIETG

#5

SPMRIH

#6

CBOORN

#7

ELIRKL

#8

RKEEAU

#9

75

CODE LETTER LAUGHS: RIDDLES

What do you call a snowman vacationing in the Bahamas?

DALPEUD

A ▉ P U D D L E

Unscramble the mixed-up letters to spell the answers to the riddles. Complete Code Letters instructions on pages 2 and 3.

RIDDLE: When it rains cats and dogs, what do you step into?

P S O D L E O

#1 [ ][ ][ ][◇][ ][ ][ ]

RIDDLE: What kind of ribbon do politicians use?

E D E T A P R

#2 [ ][ ][ ][◇][▉][ ][△][ ][ ]

RIDDLE: How do undertakers speak?

R A V Y G E L

#3 [ ][ ][ ][△][☆][ ][ ][♣]

Continued on next page.

Pat Sajak's **MIXED-UP MADNESS**

RIDDLE: What grows larger the more you take away?

L A H E O

#4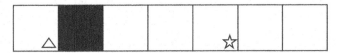

RIDDLE: What has a big mouth but can't talk?

R V A R I E

#5

RIDDLE: What flies when it's on and floats when it's off?

E F A R T H A E

#6

RIDDLE: What gets harder to catch the faster you run?

O Y U R R E H B A T

#7

HOW DO YOU RANK?	0 - 1 completely filled in = F 2 completely filled in = D 3 completely filled in = C 4 completely filled in = B	5 completely filled in = B+ 6 completely filled in = A 7 completely filled in = A+

CODE LETTER LADDER

Unscramble the mixed-up letters to spell common words. Complete Code Letters instructions on pages 2 and 3.

E M Y R C

#1

R I O F L C

#2

HOW DO YOU RANK?

0 - 1 completely filled in = F
2 - 3 completely filled in = D
4 - 5 completely filled in = C
6 completely filled in = B
7 completely filled in = A

S E N C U E R

#3

N I D I L E G T

#4

V A E A I L B A L

#5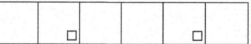

A P E C E I L Y L S

#6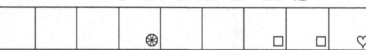

N P I T D E N E N E D

78 #7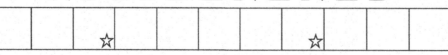

CODE LETTER LADDER

Unscramble the mixed-up letters to spell common words. Complete Code Letters instructions on pages 2 and 3.

A P O I N

#1

L J O T E S

#2

U M F L F R E

#3

T A T A L F I Y

#4

X O O I O N B U S

#5

O N C F E E N R C E

#6

F I G E N T R P I N R

#7

ACTORS AND ACTRESSES

Unscramble the mixed-up letters to spell names of
actors and actresses, as suggested by the out or
order clues. Complete Code Letters instructions
on pages 2 and 3.

NPOHJYPDNE

#1

LBLIULEALCL

#2

STAEIRYILELK

#3

VERKNEEUESA

#4

BLEJMFGDLUFO

#5

Continued on next page.

Pat Sajak's MIXED-UP MADNESS

RWDRIANEEBG

#6

NAEMESINLO

#7

HNEMKANGEAC

#8

OUT OF ORDER CLUES

Assign each answer from the puzzle to a clue below (by writing "#1," "#2," etc.).

_____ Actor born in Lebanon in 1964

_____ Actress who died in 1989 at age 78

_____ Actress who played Emma Greenway Horton in "Terms of Endearment"

_____ Actor born in Northern Ireland in 1952

_____ Actor born in Kentucky in 1963

_____ Actor who played Dr. Ian Malcolm in "Jurassic Park"

_____ Actor born in California in 1930

_____ "Cheers" star born in Kansas in 1951

HOW DO YOU RANK?

0 - 1 completely filled in = F
2 - 3 completely filled in = D
4 - 5 completely filled in = C
6 completely filled in = B
7 completely filled in = A
8 completely filled in = A+

CODE LETTER LINK LADDER

Unscramble the mixed-up letters to spell names of actors/actresses and the movies that "link" them. Complete Code Letters instructions on pages 2 and 3.

Actors / Actresses

Movies

JHSCNOACUK

HIFLTIEYDGIH

TISNRMIBOB

LMDHUALUBR

EINTECVKNROS

UPCITN

RESOENSUR

CODE LETTER LINK LADDER

Unscramble the mixed-up letters to spell names of actors/actresses and the movies that "link" them. Complete Code Letters instructions on pages 2 and 3.

Actors / Actresses

Movies

NHOITOJGV

NCGMOHMOIE

JEFNOAAND

NOTEIFVNIE

LAROTNPLDYO

NAGLILAMSOESET

YEFIDLALSL

ACTORS AND ACTRESSES

Unscramble the mixed-up letters to spell names of actors and actresses, as suggested by the out or order clues. Complete Code Letters instructions on pages 2 and 3.

KLASDORAULCBN

#1

RIJCEMRAY

#2

YSJADLHEDU

#3

DETETMLRBIE

#4

MKVILRELA

#5

Continued on next page.

Pat Sajak's MIXED-UP MADNESS

KLMRHAILAM

#6

MBLURAYIRL

#7

LTHEEUNHN

#8

OUT OF ORDER CLUES
Assign each answer from the puzzle to a clue below (by writing "#1," "#2," etc.).

_____ Actress who replaced Jodie Foster for the lead in "Double Jeopardy"

_____ Actor born in Canada who played Stanley Ipkiss in "The Mask"

_____ "Star Wars" actor born in California in 1951

_____ Actress who won a Golden Globe, an Oscar and an Emmy in the same year

_____ "Speed" star born in Virginia in 1964

_____ "Saturday Night Live" start born in 1950

_____ Actor who played Jim Morrison in "The Doors"

_____ Actress who played Mary Rose Foster in the "The Rose"

CODE LETTER SCRAMBLE 6-LETTER WORDS

Unscramble the mixed-up letters to spell common words. Complete Code Letters instructions on pages 2 and 3.

U E N R D F

#1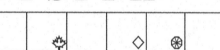

C A O N E T

#2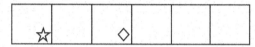

T F S I Y H

#3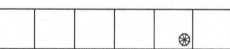

T I S E A S

#4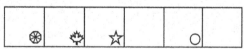

W H O R N T

#5

C R D E H N

#6

L U U R Y N

#7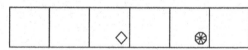

W E E T V L

#8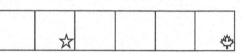

F S E Y A T

#9

CODE LETTER SCRAMBLE 6-LETTER WORDS

Unscramble the mixed-up letters to spell common words. Complete Code Letters instructions on pages 2 and 3.

GFULRA

#1

HRCCUH

#6

DGSUEL

#2

TRFUHO

#7

CUEAPT

#3

EKACRH

#8

URDISA

#4

MHAEUN

#9

MEKOSI

#5

HOW DO YOU RANK?

0 - 1 completely filled in = F	6 completely filled in = B
2 - 3 completely filled in = D	7 completely filled in = B+
4 completely filled in = C	8 completely filled in = A
5 completely filled in = C+	9 completely filled in = A+

CODE LETTER LAUGHS: RIDDLES

Unscramble the mixed-up letters to spell the answers to the riddles. Complete Code Letters instructions on pages 2 and 3.

What do you call a snowman vacationing in the Bahamas?

DALPEUD

| A | | P | U | D | D | L | E |

RIDDLE: Who makes up jokes about knitting?

I A I T W T N

#1

RIDDLE: What fish sings songs?

T H U F A I A N S

#2

RIDDLE: What keeps out bugs and shows movies?

R S C E S E N

#3

Continued on next page.

Pat Sajak's **MIXED-UP MADNESS**

RIDDLE: What has a neck but no head?

L T A B T E O

#4

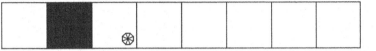

RIDDLE: What "bus" crossed the ocean?

M U S O L C B U

#5

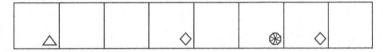

RIDDLE: The alphabet goes from A to Z. What goes from Z to A?

A E B Z R

#6

RIDDLE: What fish do knights eat?

W I O S R H S D F

#7

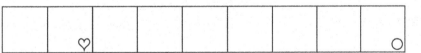

HOW DO YOU RANK?

0 - 1 completely filled in = F
2 completely filled in = D
3 completely filled in = C
4 completely filled in = B

5 completely filled in = B+
6 completely filled in = A
7 completely filled in = A+

TV SHOWS

Unscramble the mixed-up letters to spell TV show
titles, as suggested by the out or order clues. Complete
Code Letters instructions on pages 2 and 3.

PAWGINISORGN

#1

BJNASBYNOEAR

#2

ATGMCAEMH

#3

ADYFNSILNASTA

#4

DNOPVIEERC

#5

Continued on next page.

Pat Sajak's MIXED-UP MADNESS

RHKITRDEING

#6

GLHNOMOITIGN

#7

LARGIGTLEYNH

#8

OUT OF ORDER CLUES

Assign each answer from the puzzle to a clue below (by writing "#1," "#2," etc.).

_____ Popular ABC show that aired on Saturday nights after "The Love Boat"

_____ ABC detective drama/comedy that aired from 1985 to 1989

_____ ABC sitcom that aired from 1985 to 1992

_____ Show that shared its name with the U.S. state capital in which it was set

_____ Show created by and hosted by Rod Serling

_____ CBS detective drama that aired from 1973 to 1980

_____ Game show hosted by Gene Rayburn

_____ NBC show starring David Hasselhoff

HOW DO YOU RANK?

0 - 1 completely filled in = F
2 - 3 completely filled in = D
4 - 5 completely filled in = C
6 completely filled in = B
7 completely filled in = A
8 completely filled in = A+

CODE LETTER LAUGHS: RIDDLES

Unscramble the mixed-up letters to spell the answers to the riddles. Complete Code Letters instructions on pages 2 and 3.

What do you call a snowman vacationing in the Bahamas?

DALPEUD

| A | ■ | P | U | D | D | L | E |

RIDDLE: Dogs have fleas. What do sheep have?

E L E F E C

#1 | | ◇ | | | | □ | |

RIDDLE: What kind of tables do people eat?

E B E E T A L V S G

#2 | | | | △ | | | | 🍁 | | | |

RIDDLE: What flower is happiest?

L A G D I O A A L

#3 | | ■ | | △ | | | | | | | |

92

Continued on next page.

RIDDLE: What is the brightest fish?

UHASINFS

#4

RIDDLE: What do you call cattle that sit on the grass?

RFOEUGNBED

#5

RIDDLE: What did the tired shrub say to the other shrub?

MABUISEDH

#6

RIDDLE: What kind of person is fed up with people?

BNACNAILA

#7

HOW DO YOU RANK?	0 - 1 completely filled in = F	5 completely filled in = B+
	2 completely filled in = D	6 completely filled in = A
	3 completely filled in = C	7 completely filled in = A+
	4 completely filled in = B	

CODE LETTER LADDER

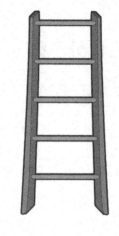

Unscramble the mixed-up letters to spell common words. Complete Code Letters instructions on pages 2 and 3.

HOW DO YOU RANK?

0 - 1 completely filled in = F
2 - 3 completely filled in = D
4 - 5 completely filled in = C
6 completely filled in = B
7 completely filled in = A

F N I L A

#1 ☐☐☐☐☐

S F I H I N

#2 ☐☐☐☐☐☐

O I U T R N E

#3 ☐☐☐☐☐☐☐

N K N D I L I G

#4 ☐☐☐☐☐☐☐☐

E S S N E E M G R

#5 ☐☐☐☐☐☐☐☐☐

H N O E N M P E O N

#6 ☐☐☐☐☐☐☐☐☐☐

A B E R M A R S E D S

94 #7 ☐☐☐☐☐☐☐☐☐☐☐

CODE LETTER LADDER

Unscramble the mixed-up letters to spell common words. Complete Code Letters instructions on pages 2 and 3.

#1 — BLOBY

#2 — SPLIHO

#3 — HASAEMD

#4 — PLDOMITA

#5 — SDSPLEIEA

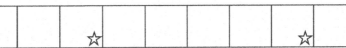

#6 — UMRAICLUSO

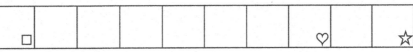

#7 — SIPIESSIMTC

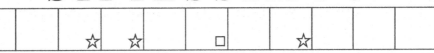

MOVIES

Unscramble the mixed-up letters to spell movie titles, as suggested by the out or order clues. Complete Code Letters instructions on pages 2 and 3.

RASAWSRT

#1

AIGCCOH

#2

NEHOOAEML

#3

GMARADNDOE

#4

ETRUIGTR

#5

Continued on next page.

Pat Sajak's MIXED-UP MADNESS

SIOTOET

#6

LDAANID

#7

TLNHTNILGIO

#8

OUT OF ORDER CLUES
Assign each answer from the puzzle to a clue below (by writing "#1," "#2," etc.).

_____ 1990 movie written by John Hughes and directed by Chris Columbus

_____ 1982 movie starring Dustin Hoffman

_____ 2002 "Best Picture" Oscar winner

_____ 1990 movie in which Bruce Willis played Harry Stamper

_____ 1992 animated movie

_____ 1977 blockbuster

_____ 1999 movie starring Julia Roberts

_____ 1969 starring John Wayne

HOW DO YOU RANK?

0 - 1 completely filled in = F
2 - 3 completely filled in = D
4 - 5 completely filled in = C
6 completely filled in = B
7 completely filled in = A
8 completely filled in = A+

RHYMES WITH...

GO --- NO
TON --- FUN
BACK --- STACK
STUCK --- TRUCK
MISTER --- SISTER
SCANDAL --- SANDAL

Unscramble the mixed-up letters to spell common words, as suggested by the out of order clues. Complete Code Letters instructions on pages 2 and 3.

MIXED-UP ANSWER   **ANSWER**

#1 LTLIHYG

#2 REDEATS

#3 PONAITP

#4 CFUINNTO

#5 CTANTIOR

#6 SELDESES

#7 AGAMRIER

Continued on next page.

Pat Sajak's MIXED-UP MADNESS

#8 LTHTORTE

| | ♣ | | ◇ | | | | ■ |

#9 APCRCOTK

| | | | | | | ◇ | ■ |

#10 RMERBMEE

| | | ♡ | | ♡ | | ■ |

OUT OF ORDER CLUES
Assign each answer from the puzzle to a clue below (by writing "#1," "#2," etc.).

_____ Rhymes with NEAREST

_____ Rhymes with JACKPOT

_____ Rhymes with DECEMBER

_____ Rhymes with JUNCTION

_____ Rhymes with ANOINT

_____ Rhymes with SLIGHTLY

_____ Rhymes with BOTTLE

_____ Rhymes with CARRIAGE

_____ Rhymes with FACTION

_____ Rhymes with NEEDLESS

HOW DO YOU RANK?
0 - 1 completely filled in = F
2 - 3 completely filled in = D
4 - 5 completely filled in = C
6 completely filled in = B
7 completely filled in = B+
8 completely filled in = A-
9 completely filled in = A
10 completely filled in = A+

MATH

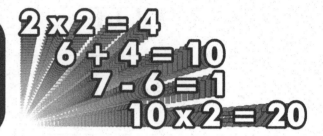

$$2 \times 2 = 4$$
$$6 + 4 = 10$$
$$7 - 6 = 1$$
$$10 \times 2 = 20$$

Unscramble the mixed-up letters to spell out correct mathematical equations that fit into the answer boxes. Complete Code Letters instructions on pages 2 and 3.

FOR EXAMPLE:

NONTEOEOW

O N E + O N E = T W O

GEEIHNEHOTIGT

#1 ☐ ☐ ☐ ⊛ ☐ ☐ × ☐ ☐ ☐ = ☐ ☐ ⊛ ☐ ☐

LNEIFIEEXVESV

#2 ☐ ☐ ☐ △ + ☐ ○ ☐ ☐ = ☐ ☐ ☐ ☐ ☐ ☐ ☐

FTOUWOUFROOTWR

#3 ☐ ♣ ☐ − ☐ ☐ ♣ = ☐ ○ ☐ ☐ − ☐ ○ ☐ ☐

TVETELEEWOELWNV

#4 ☐ ♣ ☐ ☐ ☐ ÷ ☐ ♣ ☐ ☐ ☐ = ☐ ☐ ☐

Continued on next page.

Pat Sajak's MIXED-UP MADNESS

FNHEOEIEEEOTRVN

#5 ☐☐☐ + ☐☐☐ = ⊙☐☐ − ☐☐☐☐

TNAEIETWGOEVNOENO

#6 ☐☐☐ − ☐♣☐ = ☐☐✳☐☐☐☐   ☐☐☐

RIGHFTNYOTUTEYEW

#7 ☐☐✳☐☐ ÷ ☐⊙☐ = ☐☐♣☐☐☐

TNTRTEZNTNEOEWEY

#8 ☐☐☐ + ☐☐☐ = ☐♣☐☐☐☐ + ☐☐☐

RITSTTYITIYHYTXRH

#9 ☐☐☐☐☐☐☐ + ☐☐☐☐☐☐☐ = ☐☐△☐☐

FWOVTOOUTELEURWFR

#10 ☐♣☐ × ⊙☐☐ = ☐♣☐☐☐ − ⊙☐☐

CELEBRITY BIRTHDAYS

Unscramble the mixed-up letters to spell names of celebrities, as suggested by their birthdays. Complete Code Letters instructions on pages 2 and 3.

BIRTHDAY	CELEBRITY

#1 12-4-1949

F I S D B E J F E G R

#2 9-22-1961

T A O S O I B C T

#3 2-17-1954

N E U S O R R E S

#4 2-26-1932

H N A H J Y C S N O

#5 2-18-1957

N V E W T I H N A A

CELEBRITY BIRTHDAYS

Unscramble the mixed-up letters to spell names of celebrities, as suggested by their birthdays. Complete Code Letters instructions on pages 2 and 3.

BIRTHDAY	CELEBRITY

#1 7-22-1940

L B X E R E K T E A

#2 11-30-1929

R L K C A C I K D

#3 11-19-1961

E R Y N A M G

#4 1-5-1946

N E O A N T K D E I A

#5 8-3-1940

R N E M H E N S A I T

CODE LETTER LAUGHS: RIDDLES

What do you call a snowman vacationing in the Bahamas?

DALPEUD

| A | | P | U | D | D | L | E |

Unscramble the mixed-up letters to spell the answers to the riddles. Complete Code Letters instructions on pages 2 and 3.

RIDDLE: What do you call a sunburn on your stomach?

O P T O A R S T

#1

RIDDLE: What do liars do after they die?

L E I S L T I L

#2

RIDDLE: Who can marry a lot of wives and still be single?

N A I S M R I T E

#3

Continued on next page.

Pat Sajak's MIXED-UP MADNESS

RIDDLE: What do you call it when pigs do their laundry?

H A O H W S G

#4 | | | ♡ | | 🍁 | | |

RIDDLE: What kind of jokes did Einstein make?

S W C E A C I R K S

#5 | | | | | △ | | 🍁 | △ | |

RIDDLE: What two words have thousands of letters in them?

F O E S P F T O I C

#6 | □ | | | | ■ | | | | | △ | |

RIDDLE: What is a stupid ant?

G N I O R N T A

#7 | | ♡ | | | | 🍁 | | |

HOW DO YOU RANK?

0 - 1 completely filled in = F
2 completely filled in = D
3 completely filled in = C
4 completely filled in = B

5 completely filled in = B+
6 completely filled in = A
7 completely filled in = A+

RHYMES WITH...

GO --- NO
TON --- FUN
BACK --- STACK
STUCK --- TRUCK
MISTER --- SISTER
SCANDAL --- SANDAL

Unscramble the mixed-up letters to spell common words, as suggested by the out of order clues. Complete Code Letters instructions on pages 2 and 3.

MIXED-UP ANSWER	ANSWER
#1 EITFNGM	
#2 EDCOKWL	
#3 CGSIOURA	
#4 ASPETANH	
#5 DNGUEROR	
#6 MBANEETS	
#7 BLCSBEIR	

Continued on next page.

Continued from previous page.

Pat Sajak's MIXED-UP MADNESS

#8 NSEBAIRTN

| ☆ | ✳ | | | | | | | | ■ |

#9 NGETMAEIR

| △ | | | □ | | | ✳ | | ■ |

#10 SBALEESML

| ☆ | | ✳ | □ | | | | | ■ |

OUT OF ORDER CLUES

Assign each answer from the puzzle to a clue below (by writing "#1," "#2," etc.).

_____ Rhymes with TERMINATE

_____ Rhymes with PIGMENT

_____ Rhymes with FLOUNDER

_____ Rhymes with DEADLOCK

_____ Rhymes with SPACIOUS

_____ Rhymes with PLEASANT

_____ Rhymes with DRIBBLE

_____ Rhymes with NAMELESS

_____ Rhymes with CANNISTER

_____ Rhymes with CASEMENT

HOW DO YOU RANK?
0 - 1 completely filled in = F
2 - 3 completely filled in = D
4 - 5 completely filled in = C
6 completely filled in = B
7 completely filled in = B+
8 completely filled in = A-
9 completely filled in = A
10 completely filled in = A+

TV SHOWS

Unscramble the mixed-up letters to spell TV show titles, as suggested by the out or order clues. Complete Code Letters instructions on pages 2 and 3.

TOGLRANU

#1

NARSENEO

#2

WGTSEETINHW

#3

ESFIPETKNCEC

#4

CSOTPNAEILS

#5

Continued on next page.

Pat Sajak's MIXED-UP MADNESS

VIAIMEICM

#6

HDTEICEBW

#7

RITDSEEM

#8

OUT OF ORDER CLUES
Assign each answer from the puzzle to a clue below (by writing "#1," "#2," etc.).

_____ Popular ABC sitcom that aired from 1988 to 1997

_____ CBS show created by the "Master of Disaster," Irwin Allen

_____ Popular ABC sitcom that aired from 1964 to 1972

_____ Spinoff that aired from 1977 to 1982

_____ CBS drama set in Rome, Wisconsin

_____ Show featuring a talking quadruped

_____ Police drama set in South Florida

_____ NBC drama set in Washington, D.C.

109

CODE LETTER LADDER

Unscramble the mixed-up letters to spell common words. Complete Code Letters instructions on pages 2 and 3.

N B L D O

#1

L B A L T O

#2

X T E T R E U

#3

E K E P S K E A

#4

P E B S E R A D D

#5

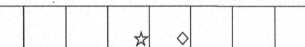

E T I M C U L U S O

#6

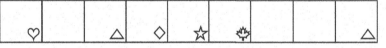

H R S H O T N A E D D

110 #7

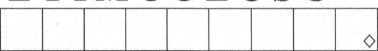

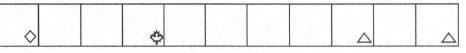

CODE LETTER LADDER

Unscramble the mixed-up letters to spell common words. Complete Code Letters instructions on pages 2 and 3.

A O M W N

#1

G D E I T S

#2

C I A E E V H

#3

R C T O B S U T

#4

N C O W N U T D O

#5

C M S C O A P I H L

#6

E U O M T R I O R I S

#7

111

Pat Sajak's **MIXED-UP MADNESS** # **74**

ADJECTIVES

BRIGHT SUNNY WARM

Unscramble the mixed-up letters to spell adjectives, as suggested by the out of order clues. Complete Code Letters instructions on pages 2 and 3.

#1 N U F Y N

#2 D R H O I R

#3 S L Z O U E A

#4 N C I R O C H

#5 B L L O A E V

#6 T Y O N B U A

#7 L C F O F U R E

112

Continued on next page.

Pat Sajak's MIXED-UP MADNESS

#8 E N E I C F I T F

#9 X U O N I S O B O

#10 R O W E U L N F D

OUT OF ORDER CLUES

Assign each answer from the puzzle to a clue below (by writing "#1," "#2," etc.).

_____ A word that could be used to describe a car that gets good gas mileage

_____ A word that could be used to describe a person who won't take no for an answer

_____ A word that could be used to describe a person who is extremely eager, committed and enthusiastic

_____ A word that could be used to describe a very bad, shocking situation

_____ A word that could be used to describe a person that everyone seems to really like

_____ A word that could be used to describe a life jacket

_____ A word that could be used to describe a person with a loud mouth who's always talking back

_____ A word that could be used to describe an illness that continues for a long time

_____ A word that could be used to describe a comedian

_____ A word that could be used to describe something that is fantastic

HOW DO YOU RANK?

0 - 1 completely filled in = F
2 - 3 completely filled in = D
4 - 5 completely filled in = C
6 completely filled in = B
7 completely filled in = B+
8 completely filled in = A-
9 completely filled in = A
10 completely filled in = A+

113

MOVIES

Unscramble the mixed-up letters to spell movie titles, as suggested by the out or order clues. Complete Code Letters instructions on pages 2 and 3.

TAOREHODPN

#1

MOAGFEODENW

#2

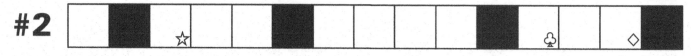

TNAAERICEUBMAY

#3

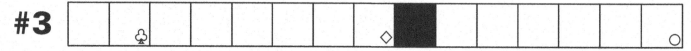

LANIELHNA

#4

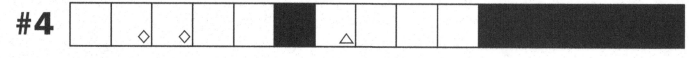

MRTENWOAYPT

#5

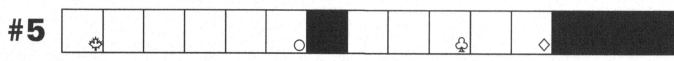

Continued on next page.

Pat Sajak's MIXED-UP MADNESS

AYCAAWTS

#6

NCIWNTOAH

#7

RNAIOEOERCF

#8

OUT OF ORDER CLUES
Assign each answer from the puzzle to a clue below (by writing "#1," "#2," etc.).

_____ 1999 movie in which Kevin Spacey played Lester Burnham

_____ 1989 movie directed by Ron Howard

_____ 1990 movie in which Julia Roberts played Vivian Ward

_____ 1992 movie directed by Rob Reiner and written by Aaron Sorkin

_____ 1997 movie in which Glenn Close played a U.S. vice president

_____ 1974 movie starring Jack Nicholson

_____ 2000 movie starring Tom Hanks

_____ 1977 "Best Picture" Oscar winner

HOW DO YOU RANK?
0 - 1 completely filled in = F
2 - 3 completely filled in = D
4 - 5 completely filled in = C
6 completely filled in = B
7 completely filled in = A
8 completely filled in = A+

115

Pat Sajak's MIXED-UP MADNESS #76

MATH

$2 \times 2 = 4$
$6 + 4 = 10$
$7 - 6 = 1$
$10 \times 2 = 20$

Unscramble the mixed-up letters to spell out correct mathematical equations that fit into the answer boxes. Complete Code Letters instructions on pages 2 and 3.

FOR EXAMPLE:

NOTLSWOEOPNEU

| O | N | E | | P | L | U | S | | O | N | E | = | T | W | O |

NETELFIPFIUVVES

#1 [ ][ ][ ][ ][ ] [ ][ ][♣][ ] [ ][ ][ ][ ][ ] = [ ][ ][ ]

RTWEOTIOSWOFUMT

#2 [ ][ ][⚜][ ] [ ][ ][ ][ ][ ][ ] [ ][ ][ ][⚜] = [ ][⚜][♣][ ]

NMOEIUSONEERONZ

#3 [⚜][ ][ ] [ ][ ][ ][♣][ ] [⚜][ ][ ][ ] = [ ][□][ ][ ][⚜]

NTEPNLTSENTWEYTU

#4 [ ][ ][ ] [ ][ ][♣][ ] [ ][ ][ ] = [ ][ ][ ][ ][ ][ ]

Continued on next page.

Pat Sajak's MIXED-UP MADNESS

UNSIPLTSREIEEHNX

#5 ▢▢▢⊛ ▢▢▢♣ ▢▢▢▢▢▢ = ▢▢▢▢

SSVNEIMUFIETNOVEW

#6 ▢▢▢▢▢▢ ▢▢▢▢♣▢ ▢▢▢▢ = ▢▢🍁

FTOMTIEOHUSREITWG

#7 ▢▢▢🍁 ▢▢▢▢▢▢ ▢▢🍁♣ = ▢▢▢♡▢▢

NFPVIUELSIELSEVXE

#8 ▢▢▢▢ ▢▢▢♣▢ ▢▢▢⊛ = ▢▢▢▢▢▢

GREITIMNHSUEITEOGZH

#9 ▢▢♡▢▢ ▢▢▢▢♣▢ ▢▢▢♡▢▢ = ▢□▢▢🍁

NXNIELNPSUEESVIETNES

#10 ▢▢▢▢▢ ▢▢▢♣ ▢▢▢▢▢▢ = ▢▢⊛▢▢▢

CODE LETTER LINK LADDER

Unscramble the mixed-up letters to spell names of actors/actresses and the movies that "link" them. Complete Code Letters instructions on pages 2 and 3.

Actors / Actresses

Movies

ULVEALDRBRTO

ONHMEPOENN

ROLTAHJOATVN

HOYSREGTT

USROERNES

KOBATURE

PESCNVIKEYA

CODE LETTER LINK LADDER

Unscramble the mixed-up letters
to spell names of actors/actresses
and the movies that "link" them.
Complete Code Letters instructions
on pages 2 and 3.

Actors / Actresses

Movies

S N T E C V K I E N R O

R O E D R L A T W W

P O P H N E I D N S R E

L E V T V L E B U E

R U E D N R L A A

S C U R P I R J S A A K

F E L G L D U B F J M O

ACTORS AND ACTRESSES

Unscramble the mixed-up letters to spell names of actors and actresses, as suggested by the out or order clues. Complete Code Letters instructions on pages 2 and 3.

OXYCTNREOUC

#1

NAPICOLA

#2

RIONRNYEWDA

#3

GRIAHREERDC

#4

DERNNARAERBSF

#5

Continued on next page.

Pat Sajak's **MIXED-UP MADNESS**

GIJAEILNLENOA

#6

MUBILLLANLP

#7

AHMGETRRAHAHE

#8

OUT OF ORDER CLUES
Assign each answer from the puzzle to a clue below (by writing "#1," "#2," etc.).

_____ Actor whose middle name is Tiffany

_____ Actress who shares her last name with a truck rental company

_____ Actor who played President Thomas J. Whitmore in "Independence Day"

_____ "Friends" star born in Alabama in 1964

_____ Jon Voight's daughter

_____ Actor born in New York City in 1940

_____ Actress born in Wisconsin in 1970

_____ Actor who played Rick O'Connel in "The Mummy"

HOW DO YOU RANK?

0 - 1 completely filled in = F
2 - 3 completely filled in = D
4 - 5 completely filled in = C
6 completely filled in = B
7 completely filled in = A
8 completely filled in = A+

CODE LETTER LAUGHS: RIDDLES

What do you call a snowman vacationing in the Bahamas?

DALPEUD

A ▮ P U D D L E

Unscramble the mixed-up letters to spell the answers to the riddles. Complete Code Letters instructions on pages 2 and 3.

RIDDLE: What canine keeps the best time?

H G A C D O W A T

#1

| | ▮ | | ♣ | | | △ | ▮ | | ♡ | |

RIDDLE: What do you get if you cross a snowman with a vampire?

T F T B E O I R S

#2

| ◇ | | ♡ | | | | | |

RIDDLE: What do prisoners use to call each other?

N E C L H O E S P L

#3

| | | | ▮ | | △ | ♡ | | | |

Continued on next page.

Pat Sajak's **MIXED-UP MADNESS**

RIDDLE: What runs around a baseball field but doesn't move?

N A C E E F

#4

RIDDLE: Why did the tree go to the dentist?

C N R O T A A L O

#5

RIDDLE: What do bulls do when they go shopping?

G H E H A R E C T Y

#6

RIDDLE: What is a tornado's favorite game?

R S I T E W T

#7

HOW DO YOU RANK?

0 - 1 completely filled in = F	5 completely filled in = B+
2 completely filled in = D	6 completely filled in = A
3 completely filled in = C	7 completely filled in = A+
4 completely filled in = B	

CODE LETTER LADDER

Unscramble the mixed-up letters to spell common words. Complete Code Letters instructions on pages 2 and 3.

#1 O Y H N E

#2 H T I E R V

#3 T A T E P T M

#4 G I M F U T E A

#5 N I V R E T O N Y

#6 G H L A H F S L I T

124 #7 A E R M P E I C T N D

CODE LETTER LADDER

Unscramble the mixed-up letters to spell common words. Complete Code Letters instructions on pages 2 and 3.

M E Y P T

#1

G A C F I N

#2

A B L F O I C

#3

O V L I T C Y E

#4

N E D O E S E B L

#5

R C E R T S E O P T

#6

A M O M E C U I N T C

#7

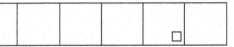

TV SHOWS

Unscramble the mixed-up letters to spell TV show titles, as suggested by the out or order clues. Complete Code Letters instructions on pages 2 and 3.

#1 ARSUEMNP

#2 HFOLSLUEU

#3 WSTEOSBCYHOH

#4 TBTLOEEOAHV

#5 HWABATCY

Continued on next page.

Continued from previous page.

Pat Sajak's MIXED-UP MADNESS

DOGOIMSET

#6

LDTEODPOCUEH

#7

HSJSMTOOETU

#8

OUT OF ORDER CLUES
Assign each answer from the puzzle to a clue below (by writing "#1," "#2," etc.).

_____ Show set on the beaches of Southern California

_____ Sitcom featuring the Olsen twins

_____ Show based on a movie which was based on a play

_____ The #1 show on TV for five straight years

_____ Show set at the offices of *Blush* magazine

_____ Show based on a comic book character

_____ ABC show that aired from 1977 to 1986

_____ Show that was a spinoff of "Maude"

MATH

$$2 \times 2 = 4$$
$$6 + 4 = 10$$
$$7 - 6 = 1$$
$$10 \times 2 = 20$$

Unscramble the mixed-up letters to spell out correct mathematical equations that fit into the answer boxes. Complete Code Letters instructions on pages 2 and 3.

FOR EXAMPLE:

NONTEOEOW

$$\boxed{O}\boxed{N}\boxed{E} + \boxed{O}\boxed{N}\boxed{E} = \boxed{T}\boxed{W}\boxed{O}$$

FENVOIEIEFV

#1 ☐☆☐☐ ÷ ☐☆☐☐☐ = ☐☐○☐

RTUGEIOFOWTH

#2 ☐☐☐☐⊛☐ ÷ ☐☆☐☐☐ = ☐☐☐

EENITWNLEENVO

#3 ☐○☐☐○ + ☐☐☐ = ☐☐☐☐☐○

GFOROHUEITFUR

#4 ☐☆☐☐ + ☐☆☐☐ = ☐☐☐☐⊛☐

Continued on next page.

Pat Sajak's MIXED-UP MADNESS

R N E F I E O T U W T Y V F

#5 ☐ ☆ ☐ ☐ ☐ × ☐ ☆ ☐ ☐ ☐ = ☐ ☐ ☐ ☐ ○ ☐ ☐

N E S I O I E O D S Z X N X

#6 ☐ ☐ ☐ + ☐ ☐ ☐ = ☐ ☐ ○ ☐   ☐ ☐ ☐ ☐ ☐ ○

R T N S I S E E T H I E N X E V

#7 ☐ ☐ ☐ + ☐ ☐ ☐ ☐ ☐ ○ = ☐ ✳ ☐ ☐ ☐ ☐ ☐ ○

T L W E V N O H I E E E R N T E T

#8 ☐ ☐ ☐ ☐ ☐ ☐ ○ + ☐ ☐ ☐ = ☐ ✳ ☐ ☐ ☐ ☐ ☐ ○

T O E D N U T H R D E N E N E N

#9 ☐ ☐ ○ ✳ ☐ ☐ ○ ☐ ☐ ÷ ☐ ☐ ○ = ☐ ☐ ○

X S I S E I F V X E V E S I N

#10 ☐ ☐ ☐ + ☐ ☐ ☐ = ☆ ☐ ☐ ☐ + ☐ ☐ ☐ ☐ ○

HOW DO YOU RANK?	0 - 1 completely filled in = F	7 completely filled in = B+
	2 - 3 completely filled in = D-	8 completely filled in = A-
	4 - 5 completely filled in = C	10 completely filled in = A+
	6 completely filled in = B	

129

MOVIES

Unscramble the mixed-up letters to spell movie titles, as suggested by the out or order clues. Complete Code Letters instructions on pages 2 and 3.

TTGHSINE

#1

ODLGITARA

#2

DBRUWAARYIEN

#3

CTAISISTNINCB

#4

DIPHHAAELILP

#5

Continued on next page.

Pat Sajak's MIXED-UP MADNESS

PRMIOIYTERNOTR

#6

LTCIOFYGESAN

#7

LBTNDUREALH

#8

OUT OF ORDER CLUES
Assign each answer from the puzzle to a clue below (by writing "#1," "#2," etc.).

_____ 1999 movie in which Julia Roberts played Maggie Carpenter

_____ 1993 movie in which Tom Hanks won a "Best Actor" Oscar

_____ 2000 "Best Picture" Oscar winner

_____ 1998 movie in which Meg Ryan played Dr. Maggie Rice

_____ 1965 James Bond movie

_____ 1973 movie set in 1930s Chicago

_____ 1992 movie starring Michael Douglas

_____ 2002 movie directed by Steven Spielberg

HOW DO YOU RANK?

0 - 1 completely filled in = F
2 - 3 completely filled in = D
4 - 5 completely filled in = C
6 completely filled in = B
7 completely filled in = A
8 completely filled in = A+

131

ACTORS AND ACTRESSES

Unscramble the mixed-up letters to spell names of actors and actresses, as suggested by the out or order clues. Complete Code Letters instructions on pages 2 and 3.

EAHSOSOTNRN

#1

WLERUILISBC

#2

DOTINESWOLACT

#3

HNACJNOILKSOC

#4

YREEIMOSJNR

#5

Continued on next page.

Pat Sajak's MIXED-UP MADNESS

RTDAGORKIDEM

#6 ♡ ♣ △ ◇

RGETRIAR

#7 ♣ ◇ ♡

KMJOCNLOHVAIH

#8 ☆ △ 🍁 ☆

OUT OF ORDER CLUES
Assign each answer from the puzzle to a clue below (by writing "#1," "#2," etc.).

_____ Actress born in Canada in 1948

_____ Actress who played Ginger McKenna in "Casino"

_____ Actor born in West Germany in 1955

_____ Actor who played Col. Nathan R. Jessep in "A Few Good Men"

_____ Actress who played Caroline Butler in "Mr. Mom"

_____ Award-winning actor/director born in San Francisco

_____ Actor who played Lennie Small in "Of Mice and Men"

_____ Actor born in England in 1948

HOW DO YOU RANK?
0 - 1 completely filled in = F
2 - 3 completely filled in = D
4 - 5 completely filled in = C
6 completely filled in = B
7 completely filled in = A
8 completely filled in = A+

CODE LETTER LINK LADDER

Unscramble the mixed-up letters
to spell names of actors/actresses
and the movies that "link" them.
Complete Code Letters instructions
on pages 2 and 3.

Actors / Actresses

Movies

SIBGEMLNO

TLAOPWELAHNE

NELORNAYDVG

NRNOYADGCAN

NVLKEIKIEN

LIWDDWTWLIES

WMTSILILH

CODE LETTER LINK LADDER

Unscramble the mixed-up letters to spell names of actors/actresses and the movies that "link" them. Complete Code Letters instructions on pages 2 and 3.

Actors / Actresses

Movies

UEBWILCRLIS

OFINILPPUCT

NHJOATAOLRVT

KBSURENLCYUM

AWROUDKSLI

ZYSTINAALEH

ARSYLLBYILCT

CODE LETTER LAUGHS: RIDDLES

Unscramble the mixed-up letters to spell the answers to the riddles. Complete Code Letters instructions on pages 2 and 3.

What do you call a snowman vacationing in the Bahamas?

DALPEUD

A		P	U	D	D	L	E

RIDDLE: What's a rabbit's favorite game?

T S O C P H O C H

#1

RIDDLE: What do you get if you put a snowman in a haunted house?

R C I C E E S M S A

#2

RIDDLE: What do cats call their grandfather?

A R W G A P N D

#3

Continued on next page.

RIDDLE: What do you get when you cross a giant with a skunk?

BAIGNTIKS

#4

RIDDLE: What did the spider make on the computer?

TSABEIEW

#5

RIDDLE: What can run but can't walk?

CAAUTFE

#6

RIDDLE: What can be taken before you even get it?

ROYRUITUEPC

#7

HOW DO YOU RANK?

0 - 1 completely filled in = F
2 completely filled in = D
3 completely filled in = C
4 completely filled in = B
5 completely filled in = B+
6 completely filled in = A
7 completely filled in = A+

CODE LETTER LADDER

Unscramble the mixed-up letters to spell common words. Complete Code Letters instructions on pages 2 and 3.

CTIKR

#1

ERLARY

#2

DIWEDNG

#3

URLOEREV

#4

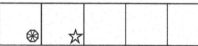

AEMENMUST

#5

MGVNRNTEOE

#6

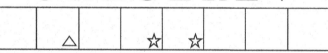

NAEGIOTOTIN

138 #7

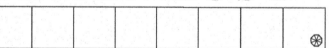

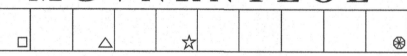

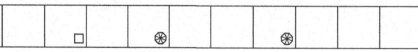

CODE LETTER LADDER

Unscramble the mixed-up letters to spell common words. Complete Code Letters instructions on pages 2 and 3.

OGRPU

#1

RENTYS

#2

REABRIR

#3

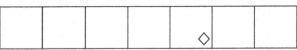

MIWMIGNS

#4

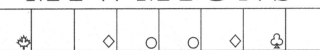

SASAITTNS

#5

ETNAATHMTC

#6

TNORAIELIAZ

#7

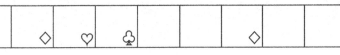

139

MOVIES

Unscramble the mixed-up letters to spell movie titles, as suggested by the out or order clues. Complete Code Letters instructions on pages 2 and 3.

KTAMSEH

#1

WHASTIHED

#2

NSIAARY

#3

TETHADGUERA

#4

AGUNOGDODYHR

#5

Continued on next page.

Pat Sajak's MIXED-UP MADNESS

HBEINOORVICRK

#6

SYOTYTRO

#7

ERMSICIVRYT

#8

OUT OF ORDER CLUES
Assign each answer from the puzzle to a clue below (by writing "#1," "#2," etc.).

_____ 2005 movie starring George Clooney

_____ 1967 movie starring Anne Bancroft

_____ 2000 movie starring Julia Roberts

_____ 1974 movie starring Charles Bronson

_____ 1995 animated movie

_____ 1994 movie starring Jim Carrey

_____ 2003 movie directed by Clint Eastwood

_____ 1993 movie starring Bill Murray

HOW DO YOU RANK?
0 - 1 completely filled in = F
2 - 3 completely filled in = D
4 - 5 completely filled in = C
6 completely filled in = B
7 completely filled in = A
8 completely filled in = A+

BIRDS

Unscramble the mixed-up letters to spell types of birds. Complete Code Letters instructions on pages 2 and 3.

#1 HIFCN

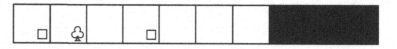

#2 LGEEA

#3 FPINUF

#4 OIPENG

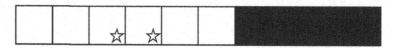

#5 EKCICNH

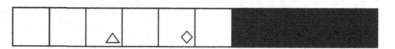

#6 CECOKAP

Continued on next page.

Pat Sajak's **MIXED-UP MADNESS**

#7 W R S A O R P

#8 A D C A N L I R

#9 L T A G R I N S

#10 U R B B E I D L

#11 N L A I O G F M

#12 S A P E A T H N

#13 A G D P R I T E R

#14 S R A A T O S B L

HOW DO YOU RANK?

0 - 1 completely filled in = F	7 completely filled in = C	11 completely filled in = B+
2 - 3 completely filled in = D-	8 completely filled in = C+	12 completely filled in = A-
4 - 5 completely filled in = D	9 completely filled in = B	13 completely filled in = A
6 completely filled in = C-	10 completely filled in = B-	14 completely filled in = A+

MATH

$$2 \times 2 = 4$$
$$6 + 4 = 10$$
$$7 - 6 = 1$$
$$10 \times 2 = 20$$

Unscramble the mixed-up letters to spell out correct mathematical equations that fit into the answer boxes. Complete Code Letters instructions on pages 2 and 3.

FOR EXAMPLE:

NOTLSWOEOPNEU

ONE PLUS ONE = TWO

S P L F O U S W O I X R T U

#1 ⊛ □ □ □   □ □ □ □ □   △ □ □ = □ □ □

S T X M S O I E X S I N I E

#2 □ □ □ □   △ □ □ □ □   □ □ □ □ = □ □ □

T M I T E I S T O E E V N F W

#3 ⊛ □ ☆ □   △ □ □ □ □   △ □ □ = △ □ □

W M F R T O T I E T U O O W S

#4 △ □ □   △ □ □ □ □   △ □ □ = ⊛ □ □ □

Continued on next page.

R W S O T U W I U O T N O F M

#5

V P I S F E L I F E E U N T V

#6

T N N R I U S H L E E I E S P X

#7

E M N T N E T I S T U N E T N W Y

#8

T F T V N P L E S E F E F I E I N U

#9

N N E I E E M T W I U N S V O N E L

#10

ACTORS AND ACTRESSES

Unscramble the mixed-up letters to spell names of actors and actresses, as suggested by the out or order clues. Complete Code Letters instructions on pages 2 and 3.

ERPATHWTERYM

#1

ADJENOANF

#2

TAUHHRGGN

#3

ULSKTURSELR

#4

AKSLAMYEAH

#5

Continued on next page.

Continued from previous page.

Pat Sajak's MIXED-UP MADNESS

HNAOTPONKISNYH

#6

RWLRSELCOESU

#7

RDSJIEOTEOF

#8

OUT OF ORDER CLUES
Assign each answer from the puzzle to a clue below (by writing "#1," "#2," etc.).

_____ Actor who played Wyatt Earp in "Tombstone"

_____ Award-winning actor born in Wales in 1937

_____ Actress who played Viola Fields in "Monster-in-Law"

_____ Actress who started career appearing in commercials at age 2

_____ "Friends" star born in Massachusetts in 1969

_____ Actress born in Mexico in 1966

_____ Actor born in England in 1960

_____ Actor born in New Zealand in 1964

147

CODE LETTER LAUGHS: RIDDLES

What do you call a snowman vacationing in the Bahamas?

DALPEUD

| A | | P | U | D | D | L | E |

Unscramble the mixed-up letters to spell the answers to the riddles. Complete Code Letters instructions on pages 2 and 3.

RIDDLE: What is a musical pickle?

POCAIOLC

#1

RIDDLE: What do you lose every time you stand up?

AOURYLP

#2

RIDDLE: What has a head but no brain?

BGCAAEAB

#3

Continued on next page.

RIDDLE: What can you serve but not eat?

LYALOVLBLEA

#4

RIDDLE: What animal never needs a haircut?

GBLEAALAED

#5

RIDDLE: What do you call a snowman in the summer?

DPAULED

#6

RIDDLE: What do you get when you cross a cheetah and a hamburger?

TAOSFODF

#7

149

CELEBRITY BIRTHDAYS

Unscramble the mixed-up letters to spell names of celebrities, as suggested by their birthdays. Complete Code Letters instructions on pages 2 and 3.

BIRTHDAY	CELEBRITY

#1 5-23-1958 A Y R D R C E W E

#2 4-19-1968 E Y H L U D J D S A

#3 4-12-1956 D R A I C G N Y A A

#4 11-6-1946 L D I F L L S Y A E

#5 8-14-1966 H L R E Y R B A E L

CELEBRITY BIRTHDAYS

Unscramble the mixed-up letters to spell names of celebrities, as suggested by their birthdays. Complete Code Letters instructions on pages 2 and 3.

BIRTHDAY   **CELEBRITY**

#1 9-16-1927   A K R F L T P E E

#2 6-22-1949   M R T P R E S E E L Y

#3 10-8-1943   S E A H C H V C Y E

#4 5-18-1912   R O C O R Y E P M

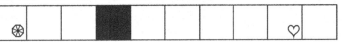

#5 6-28-1926   R B O S K E M L O

TV SHOWS

Unscramble the mixed-up letters to spell TV show titles, as suggested by the out or order clues. Complete Code Letters instructions on pages 2 and 3.

RGBIRTEOHB

#1

AHNTEWR

#2

RNTELGERONEHA

#3

RRAEGNECES

#4

EGTEFITVIHU

#5

Continued on next page.

Pat Sajak's MIXED-UP MADNESS

MLRBAEEILNRY

#6 [ ][ ][□][♡][◇][■][○][ ][ ][□][■]

HSTEOEKENM

#7 [ ][ ][ ][■][○][♡][ ][△][■]

NRPRYASOEM

#8 [ ][ ][□][□][◇][■][○][△][♡][■]

OUT OF ORDER CLUES
Assign each answer from the puzzle to a clue below (by writing "#1," "#2," etc.).

_____ Sitcom that featured a pig

_____ Show starring David Janssen

_____ CBS reality show

_____ Show set at the 12th Precinct station house

_____ Legal drama that aired from 1957 to 1966

_____ Show set in Vermont

_____ Sitcom starring a rock band

_____ TV show that began as a radio show

HOW DO YOU RANK?
0 - 1 completely filled in = F
2 - 3 completely filled in = D
4 - 5 completely filled in = C
6 completely filled in = B
7 completely filled in = A
8 completely filled in = A+

153

CODE LETTER SCRAMBLE 6-LETTER WORDS

Unscramble the mixed-up letters to spell common words. Complete Code Letters instructions on pages 2 and 3.

T E A E N G

#1

D I V E N A

#6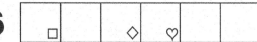

E L C I P K

#2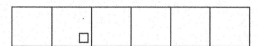

B Z A O G E

#7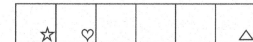

T E O T N G

#3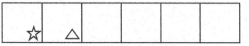

D L A E D O

#8

C E N B A O

#4

V I D S T E

#9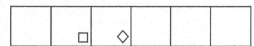

O T E R L V

#5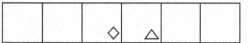

CODE LETTER SCRAMBLE
6-LETTER WORDS

Unscramble the mixed-up letters to spell common words. Complete Code Letters instructions on pages 2 and 3.

#1 ADSINL

#6 ANTTMU

#2 DCLIPA

#7 SIBYPO

#3 EGVLAR

#8 TREAMK

#4 MSEERU

#9 SKFYIR

#5 GMNUET

HOW DO YOU RANK?

0 - 1 completely filled in = F	6 completely filled in = B
2 - 3 completely filled in = D	7 completely filled in = B+
4 completely filled in = C	8 completely filled in = A
5 completely filled in = C+	9 completely filled in = A+

CODE LETTER LAUGHS: RIDDLES

Unscramble the mixed-up letters to spell the answers to the riddles. Complete Code Letters instructions on pages 2 and 3.

What do you call a snowman vacationing in the Bahamas?

DALPEUD

| A | | P | U | D | D | L | E |

RIDDLE: How do you make a walnut laugh?

UCARITPKC

#1

RIDDLE: What do you get from a dancing cow?

KIMKASESHL

#2

RIDDLE: What goes up and never comes down?

UORAYGE

#3

Continued on next page.

RIDDLE: What did the teddy bear say after it ate?

FTIMUAFEDS

#4

RIDDLE: What bird is with you at every meal?

LAALWOSW

#5

RIDDLE: What happened when the horse swallowed a dollar bill?

KUHBCEDE

#6

RIDDLE: What is a foreign ant?

RMATIONTP

#7

CODE LETTER™
CROSSWORDS #1

ACROSS CLUES

1 Buckle from heat
5 Prevail upon
9 Insulation units
14 Cookie favorite
15 Future queen?
16 "Silas Marner" novelist George
17 Play first fiddle
20 Hunting expedition
21 Valueless
22 Lucy of "Charlie's Angels"
23 Old horses
25 Vestments
27 Restrain
31 "Now I get it!"

32 Normandy invasion town
33 More compliant
37 Bough
39 Vegas headliner
41 Lovebirds' place
42 Fill to the rim
45 Wise guy
48 Hither's partner
49 Control all subordinates
52 Schematic drawing
55 TV jock Swann
56 Drop the ball
57 Chin-wipers
59 Frames
63 Be in complete control

66 Prepare for a dubbing
67 Peeping Tom, say
68 Quaffs at dart tournaments
69 Rope fiber
70 Department store department
71 Put through the paces

DOWN CLUES

1 Astounds
2 Opera staple
3 Underwater knoll
4 Baltic Sea country
5 Edgy
6 Shout from the stands
7 No Doubt vocalist Stefani
8 Guarantee
9 Straight shot
10 Chalet backdrop
11 Proof of ownership
12 Part of a front-end alignment
13 Pompous gait
18 Mild oaths
19 Have dibs on

24 Bear's cry?
26 Quicker than a flash (Abbr.)
27 "Freeze!"
28 New addition of 1803
29 It may have a gooseneck
30 Facetious tribute
34 Roundhouse result, sometimes
35 They're often inflated
36 Budget item
38 Five-time Wimbledon champ
40 Satirist Mort
43 Cuddly pet name
44 Threshing tool

46 Yellowstone attractions
47 Sea eagles
50 Ball-cap symbol
51 Two words before "note"
52 Coldcocks
53 Persian, today
54 Van Gogh setting
58 Eyelid woe
60 Food fish
61 Southwestern Indians
62 Verbal jab in the ribs
64 Actress Thompson
65 Brooder

158

BONUS PUZZLE

Complete "Code Letters" instructions on pages 2 and 3.

1 ☆	2	3	4 ✴		5	6	7 ◇	8		9	10	11	12	13 □
14					15 ✴		7 ☆			16				
17 ☆			18				□	19			✴			
20 □						21						22		
		23		◇	24 □		25		26					
27	28	29				30				□				
31				32 □				33			34	35	36	
37		38			39		40 □			41			◇	
42 ✴				43	44		45 □		46 ◇	47		48		
		49 ◇			50					51 □				
52	53	54					55							
56			57			58 □		59 □			60 □	61	62 ✴	
63		64				65			□				□	
66					67				68				□	
69 □			□		70				71		□		

159

CODE LETTER

CROSSWORDS #2

ACROSS CLUES

1 Hunk's date
5 Some desktop clutter
10 Legal reprieve
14 River to the Caspian
15 Total
16 Citizen of Hollywood
17 Convenience store partners
20 Turkish topper
21 Commission
22 Constellation member
23 "Hast thou ___ the Jabberwock?"
25 Selector of Salt Lake City, UT
27 Cuban dance

31 India and Australia, once
34 Absorbed, as an expense
35 Work up to a canter
36 Mortarboard
37 Saudi Arabia neighbor
40 Spiny plants
42 1986 pennant winner
43 Give a hard time
44 Plummet
45 Conscious mind
47 "You'd better sit down for this!"
51 Clean with a vengeance
52 OT book
53 Essentials
56 Step on it

58 PBS relative
60 Morse code "e"
61 Support for glasses
66 Hall of Fame manager Weaver
67 Like crossword puzzle entries
68 Expanse
69 Kiddie
70 Serves up the brewskis
71 Soak up some sun

DOWN CLUES

1 Enthusiasts
2 Ehud's successor in Israel
3 "La ComÈdie Humaine" author
4 Architectural add-on
5 Lion's trademark
6 Fit, but just barely
7 RNs' co-workers
8 Get more baskets than
9 Small quarrel
10 Downhill course
11 "The Way" of Chinese religion
12 Bay State cape
13 "You bet!"
18 "Otherwise ..."

19 78-card deck
24 Islamic republic
26 Invertebrate with three hearts
28 Mickey and Minnie
29 Drum contribution
30 African snakes
32 Bushed
33 Fails to retain
37 Planets, e.g.
38 Horse painter Franz
39 Petri dish mixture
41 Way around the law
42 Underground tunneler
44 Clean up, as a computer program

46 Literary style
48 Become lumpy
49 Mouthed off
50 Hat with a crown
54 Doctor's orders
55 It might be a minute
57 Splinter group
59 Profs, usually
61 Play the odds
62 Actor Milland
63 Annoy
64 Pleasurable
65 Collar

160

BONUS PUZZLE

Complete "Code Letters" instructions on pages 2 and 3.

1	2	3	4		5	6	7	8	9		10	11	12	13
14					15						16			
17				18					19					
20					21			22						
23			24			25	26			27		28	29	30
	31			32				33						
		34			35					36				
37	38	39			40	41				42				
43				44				45	46					
47			48				49			50				
51					52			53			54	55		
		56		57		58	59			60				
61	62	63			64			65						
66				67				68						
69				70				71						

161

CODE LETTER

CROSSWORDS #3

ACROSS CLUES

1 Molt
5 Classes
11 Place where many would twist
14 Bern's river
15 Certain orchestra member
16 Winner in tennis
17 Columbia River dam
19 Rm. coolers
20 Magazine income
21 1.5 volt battery size
22 Fuzzy
24 Sonny Corleone portrayer
26 Salt River dam

30 Priest and minister's cohort, in jokes
31 Andrews of "Laura"
32 Architect's pier
33 Dormant
35 Dole's running mate, 1996
37 Tennessee River dam
39 Colorado River dam (officially "Hoover")
44 Snifter part
46 Teem
47 Salad bar choice
51 Abel's nephew
53 Rhythmic cadences
54 Cowlitz River dam

56 Archipelago part
57 Mystic's board
58 Playable serves
60 Some bandits have one
62 Out of the ordinary
63 Flathead River dam
68 Half a laugh
69 Duller of the senses
70 Score after deuce, in tennis
71 Time divs.
72 Not AWOL
73 Nine-digit Ids

DOWN CLUES

1 Long adventure story
2 Not checks or credit
3 Can be easily removed by rubbing
4 Hotbed of iniquity
5 "Your Show of Shows" regular
6 On the plane
7 Old French coin
8 "Closed ___ noon" (sign)
9 Hamburg-to-Warsaw dir.
10 Jobs of computers
11 First name in ice cream
12 Hidden and difficult to see
13 100 centimos

18 "Dumb and Dumber" star
23 One of Mickey's exes
25 Sting like ___
27 Tree with yellow ribbons, in song
28 First floor apt., perhaps
29 U.S. island territory
30 Like some deals
34 Aka Simon
36 Put into print
38 Slots site
40 Clark's co-worker
41 Numbskulls
42 Joins, as an agreement
43 County streets (Abbr.)

45 Soft shoe, briefly
47 Peanut butter choice
48 More garish
49 Private stage remarks
50 N.Y.C. financial daily
52 Avoids, as an issue
55 Boorish sort
59 No, in Siberia
61 One restroom
64 New competitor of ABC and CBS
65 Autumn chill
66 Fed. audit agency
67 West. Hemisphere alliance

BONUS PUZZLE

Complete "Code Letters" instructions on pages 2 and 3.

1	2 ☆	3	4 ○		5 ◇	6	7	8	9	10		11 ☆	12	13 ♡
14					15							16		◇
17 🍁				18 ○	◇							19		◇
20		○		21						22	23	🍁		
	24 ◇		25			26	27	28	29					
30						31 ○					32			
33				34 ♡		35			36 ♡					
37		☆			38		39			40	41 ○	42	43	
			44			45		46						○
47	48	49	50		51		52		53					
54			55			◇			56					
57							58	59			60		61	
62	○	○		63	64	65	66 🍁			☆	67			
68				69		♡					70	○		
71 ☆				72		♡					73			

163

CODE LETTER™
CROSSWORDS #4

ACROSS CLUES

1 Famous tower's city
5 Public meeting
10 Manhattan neighborhood
14 Egyptian cobras
15 Kind of acid
16 Plunger's target
17 It'll get you out of bed
19 Object of worship
20 ___ cotta
21 Sign brightener
22 Renaissance name of fame
23 Oktoberfest mementos
25 Boy band
27 Light shades
30 Felt the strain?
33 Diamond bag
36 Word with state or sales
37 Like jambalaya
38 More than most
39 Puddinglike dessert
41 Pay stub?
42 Study (with "on")
44 Be subject to garnishment
45 Controversial apple spray
46 Force out
47 One of the Seven Dwarfs
49 Nametag word
51 Puzzle solving aid
55 Pitfall
57 Like some vaccines
60 Actress Garbo
61 Shrill barks
62 Dieter's treat
64 Kind of dream
65 Trunk
66 World's longest river
67 One-named New Ager
68 Goes tit-for-tat
69 It can follow the last word of this puzzle's theme

DOWN CLUES

1 Summit results, sometimes
2 Lighthouse site, perhaps
3 Future mushroom
4 Assign
5 Where achievers go
6 Fort of Jalali locale
7 Get carried away?
8 Labor groups
9 Ancient calendar units
10 Word with fiction or fair
11 Traditional
12 Derisive sound
13 Eye up and down
18 Welles' tycoon publisher
24 Ab strengthener
26 Material measure
28 21-Across, for one
29 Praise
31 Scat first name
32 Letter opener
33 Reveal
34 "Family Ties" character
35 Giddy
37 Move close to the ground
39 Reject
40 More than impress
43 Kind of diver
45 "We the Living" novelist
47 Sadness
48 Cribbage equipment
50 Upper levels
52 "As You Like It" woman
53 Location of 1-Across
54 Puts on cargo
55 Cast leader
56 Word with forest or barrel
58 Mystique
59 Part of Daffy Duck's charm
63 How-___ (instructional books)

BONUS PUZZLE

Complete "Code Letters" instructions on pages 2 and 3.

CODE NUMBER™
SUDOKU #1

"Code Numbers" instructions on page 3.

BONUS PUZZLE

CODE NUMBER™
SUDOKU #2

	3		5		○	2		△
○	△		9					
	4		7		△	8		
2		△		3			○	4
5	○			1				7
6				○		△		9
△		7			2		4	○
		○	△		6		3	
		9	○		4	△	5	

"Code Numbers" instructions on pages 3.

BONUS PUZZLE

CODE NUMBER™
SUDOKU #3

8	4		3	♡	6	△		
7	3		5	○	1		♡	
2			7		9	○		6
○		♡		5			△	
6			♡	1	△		○	9
		△		3	○	♡		
1			8	△	♡			4
	△	○	1		5		6	2
	♡		4		3		5	7

"Code Numbers" instructions on pages 3.

BONUS PUZZLE

CODE NUMBER™
SUDOKU #4

			4	9	2	☆		1
♣				☆	♣			
6	2					3	4	
	9	☆				♣		8
	☆				3			♣
8			2	7	6			☆
		♣	1		☆			
☆		3		♣		9	1	
	♣	4					☆	6
9			☆	2	8		♣	

"Code Numbers" instructions on pages 3.

BONUS PUZZLE

CODE NUMBER™
SUDOKU #5

			♥	4	○	8		
1		♥				2	5	○
	7	9		5			♥	6
	3	5				○		9
			1	○	6			♥
○				♥		6	2	
9				8		♥	7	
	8	4	○		♥			5
♥		7	9	6	2			

"Code Numbers" instructions on pages 3.

170

BONUS PUZZLE

CODE NUMBER™
SUDOKU #6

	2			7	6	4	☆	
6		☆	8			7		△
9			△		☆	5		
☆	△			9			8	
	7			2	△	☆	6	
5				☆			△	
		4	☆	△	7			9
		1			5	6		☆
☆	8	4	6			△	7	

"Code Numbers" instructions on pages 3.

BONUS PUZZLE

Pat Sajak's **CODE LETTERS**™

EDITION

TriBond #1

Use the Code Letters to help you figure out what the three things that make up each Threezer have in common. For example, "TREES, CARS, ELEPHANTS" = "They all have TRUNKS." Complete Code Letters instructions on pages 2 and 3.

THREEZER #1

A MAN, A TIRE, AN EAGLE

They can all...

THREEZER #2

A CHRISTMAS TREE, A WAR HERO, A HOUSE

They can all...

THREEZER #3

CARS, STREET GANGS, SHERWOOD FOREST

They all...

THREEZER #4

SCHOOL, ARMY, PACK

They can all be...

172

Continued on next page.

Continued from previous page.

THREEZER #5

A CASINO, A COMPUTER, FRITO LAY

They all...

THREEZER #6

A BUTTON, A SHIRT, A BARBELL

They can all...

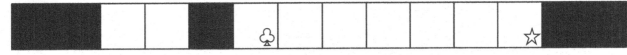

THREEZER #7

THE US. PRESIDENT, BRITISH PRIME MINISTER, A KITCHEN

They all...

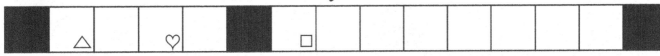

THREEZER #8

EYES, A LOAD OF LAUNDRY, EGGS

They all...

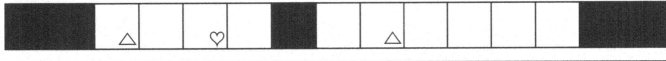

THREEZER #9

HAZEL BURKE, MRS. LIVINGSTON, ALICE NELSON

They were all...

173

Pat Sajak's **CODE LETTERS** ™

TriBond EDITION

TriBond #2

Use the Code Letters to help you figure out what the three things that make up each Threezer have in common. For example, "TREES, CARS, ELEPHANTS" = "They all have TRUNKS." Complete Code Letters instructions on pages 2 and 3.

THREEZER #1

1

THE STATUE OF LIBERTY, DIAMOND HEAD, ALCATRAZ

They're all...

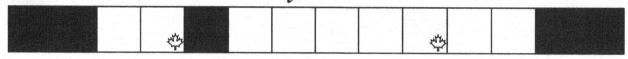

THREEZER #2

2

BILLIARD BALLS, CALLING CARDS, MAILBOXES

They all...

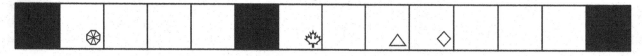

THREEZER #3

3

"GOOD GRIEF," "HELLO ANGELS," "THE DEVIL WENT DOWN TO GEORGIA..."

They're all...

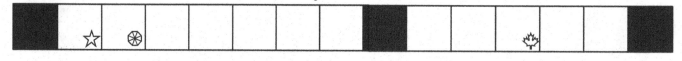

THREEZER #4

4

NURSE, LEMON, HAMMERHEAD

They're all...

Continued on next page.

THREEZER #5

A DIME, RHODE ISLAND, MERCURY (PLANET)

They're all considered...

THREEZER #6

A CONTROL, A SEWING KIT, AN ELEVATOR

They all...

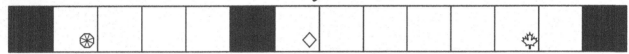

THREEZER #7

A GUN, A CAMERA, A WASHING MACHINE

They can all...

THREEZER #8

HONOLULU, CHEYENNE, TOPEKA

They're all...

THREEZER #9

A GUITAR, A GENIE BOTTLE, A FLAMINGO

They all...

Pat Sajak's CODE LETTERS™

EDITION

TriBond #3

Use the Code Letters to help you figure out what the three things that make up each Threezer have in common. For example, "TREES, CARS, ELEPHANTS" = "They all have TRUNKS." Complete Code Letters instructions on pages 2 and 3.

THREEZER #1

A CANYON, A GLASS, A BASKETBALL COURT

1

They all...

THREEZER #2

KING, BLUE, HORSESHOE,

2

They can all be...

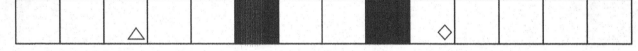

THREEZER #3

CHICAGO, ALABAMA, BOSTON

3

They're all...

THREEZER #4

FOREST, KELLY, OLIVE

4

They're all...

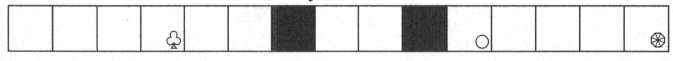

Continued on next page.

Continued from previous page.

THREEZER #5

BASEBALL GAMES, TRACK MEETS, SLEDS

They all...

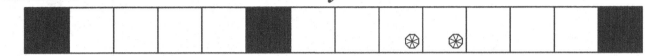

THREEZER #6

A DOCTOR, A MAILMAN, DOMINOES

They can all...

THREEZER #7

AN ELECTRIC TOASTER, A NEWBORN BABY, A PARACHUTE

They all...

THREEZER #8

A LAWYER, A LUGGAGE STORE, A LIQUOR STORE

They all...

THREEZER #9

ROMA DOWNEY, FARRAH FAWCETT, JESSICA ALBA

They all...

BONUS PUZZLES

CODE LETTER™
CROSSWORD CONNECTIONS

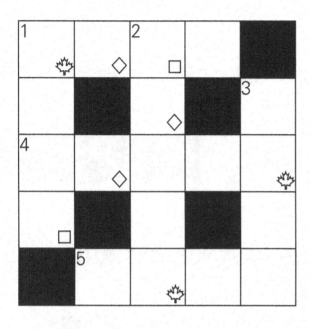

ACROSS CLUES

1 House
4 Tumble's partner
5 Gangster

DOWN CLUES

1 Injure
2 River ending
3 Swallow, swig

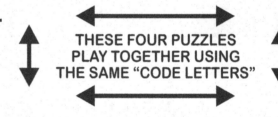

THESE FOUR PUZZLES
PLAY TOGETHER USING
THE SAME "CODE LETTERS"

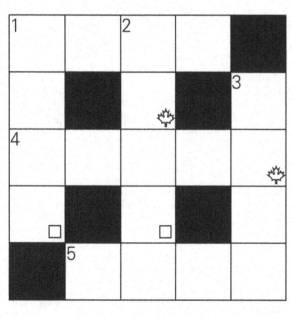

ACROSS CLUES

1 Kiss
4 Restraint
5 Small fight

DOWN CLUES

1 Tropical tree
2 Victor
3 Close

BONUS PUZZLES

CROSSWORD CONNECTIONS

ACROSS CLUES

1 Long river
4 Proprietor
5 Type of dress

DOWN CLUES

1 "Ne"
2 Language
3 Small bird

ACROSS CLUES

1 Borrowed money
4 Ancient
5 Tie

DOWN CLUES

1 Diving bird
2 Great warmth
3 Again, fresh

JOIN PAT SAJAK FOR A GAME OF . . .
PAT SAJAK'S LUCKY LETTERS™ DELUXE

FOR PC CD-ROM

Pat Sajak's Lucky Letters™ Deluxe invites gamers of all ages to be contestants in this fast-paced game that combines the excitement of a TV game show with the challenge of a word puzzle.

◆ **MORE THAN 30,000 CLUES AND ANSWERS**
◆ **SINGLE AND MULTI-PLAYER FORMATS**
◆ **THREE DIFFERENT GAME VARIATIONS**

"DELUXE" EDITION
FEATURES EXCLUSIVE
CONTENT FROM PAT

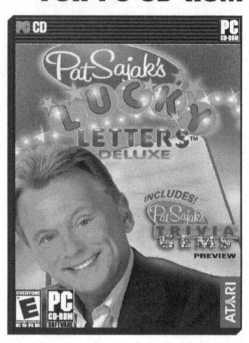

www.PatSajakGames.com

ANSWERS

#1 ALONE, SAUNA, UNION, BACON, HOUND, SLASH, YODEL, CARGO, PLANT

#2 SCOOP, WHOLE, TUMOR, BLURT, ALOUD, LOCAL, PORCH, WOULD, CRIMP

#3 GROUP, POCKET, HIDEOUT, HARDWARE, SUNFLOWER, BATTLESHIP, CONTRAPTION

#4 FRUIT, REMOVE, CHECKUP, LANDFILL, YOUNGSTER, PICKPOCKET, SIGNIFICANT

#5 SCARFACE, DIE HARD, PULP FICTION, THE GODFATHER, CONTACT, VERTIGO, THE STING, PATTON, 3, 5, 7, 2, 8, 4, 1, 6

#6 A STAIRCASE, A CHAIR, A MIRROR, ROMANS, A BALD MAN, YOUR NAME, A RULER

#7 NOISY, TRICKY, ORNERY, STRONG, VICIOUS, DISTANT, SPECIAL, DEVIOUS, LENGTHY, JEALOUS, 9, 4, 10, 1, 8, 2, 7, 5, 3, 6

#8 SIX-FOUR=TWO, ZEROxZERO=ZERO, SIX/TWO=THREE, ONE+EIGHT=NINE, TENxFIVE=FIFTY, EIGHTxZERO=ZERO, FIFTYxONE=FIFTY, NINE/THREE=THREE, ONE+ELEVEN=TWELVE, TWENTY+TEN=THIRTY

#9 TIM ALLEN, SALLY FIELD, LAURA LINNEY, GARY SINISE, DEMI MOORE, MATT DAMON, JENNIFER LOPEZ, KEVIN BACON, 3, 5, 6, 1, 7, 2, 8, 4

#10 THIRD, JUNGLE, BUTTER, SUMMIT, PASSIVE, ROYALTY, BROTHER, WEALTHY, CRUMBLE, CHEERFUL, 4, 8, 9, 10, 3, 7, 2, 1, 6, 5

#11 JOE PESCI, CASINO, SHARON STONE, BASIC INSTINCT, MICHAEL DOUGLAS, WONDER BOYS, TOBEY MAGUIRE

#12 BEN AFFLECK, PEARL HARBOR, ALEC BALDWIN, MALICE, NICOLE KIDMAN, THE PEACEMAKER, GEORGE CLOONEY

#13 DYNASTY, SEINFELD, STAR TREK, THE MUNSTERS, SURVIVOR, GUNSMOKE, AMERICAN IDOL, THE SOPRANOS, 5, 6, 1, 3, 7, 2, 8, 4

#14 KNOWN, ALPHA, MEDIC, TOTAL, MACAW, OASIS, RAVEN, BRAVE, CHAOS

#15 VOICE, TREND, MOVIE, YODEL, VINYL, SCUBA, HATCH, HELLO, BUNCH

#16 KATHY BATES, HELEN HUNT, JANE LEEVES, STEVE MARTIN, JOHN RITTER

#17 CHUCK NORRIS, JERRY REED, PAUL NEWMAN, SHELLEY LONG, ROGER MOORE

ANSWERS

#18 GROOM, MIDDLE, ICEBERG, SHOULDER, FRIGHTFUL, EXCITEMENT, PUBLICATION

#19 FLOCK, REFLEX, ORCHARD, CHESTNUT, HUMANKIND, SUSPENSION, SENTIMENTAL

#20 JURASSIC PARK, FIGHT CLUB, CASABLANCA, UNFORGIVEN, REAR WINDOW, WITNESS, JAGGED EDGE, BRAVEHEART, 3, 5, 4, 8, 1, 7, 2, 6

#21 A HORSEFLY, A TYRANT, A GOLDFISH, A SIDEWALK, RUN DOWN, TO THE DOCK, FRANKLY

#22 AIRWAY, CRYING, DENTAL, POSTAL, DEDUCT, PELLET, LESSON, PILFER, DOMINO

#23 GROCER, FRUGAL, LIMBER, BRIDLE, BECOME, KENNEL, CURSED, DETAIL, INFORM

#24 MEL GIBSON, TOM CRUISE, CARRIE FISHER, ROGER MOORE, ALEC BALDWIN, JOHN WAYNE, GLENN CLOSE, GEORGE CLOONEY, 4, 5, 1, 8, 2, 3, 6, 7

#25 A CARPET, WELL WATER, BALDNESS, A RIVER, A HAMMER, IT GETS WET, BUGS BUNNY

#26 FOUR/ONE=FOUR, ONE + THREE = FOUR, FIVE-TWO=THREE, FOUR+ZERO=FOUR, FIVE+TWO=SEVEN, ZERO-ZERO=ZERO, EIGHT/FOUR=TWO, SIXTY/TWO=THIRTY, SEVEN-ZERO=SEVEN, THREExTHREE=NINE

#27 PEYTON PLACE, HAPPY DAYS, BONANZA, MAD ABOUT YOU, FAMILY TIES, FRASIER, FAMILY FEUD, THE SIMPSONS, 3, 6, 1, 7, 2, 5, 8, 4

#28 PUSHY, BRANCH, BALCONY, BEHAVIOR, APPREHEND, STRENGTHEN, ENVIRONMENT

#29 TOXIC, RUNNER, ATTRACT, COLOSSAL, FACSIMILE, MEMBERSHIP, ARCHIPELAGO

#30 DANNY GLOVER, ED HARRIS, NICOLE KIDMAN, MERYL STREEP, DAN AYKROYD, STEVE MARTIN, EDDIE MURPHY, GOLDIE HAWN, 3, 8, 1, 6, 7, 4, 5, 2

#31 BILLY CRYSTAL, FORGET PARIS, DEBRA WINGER, BLACK WIDOW, DENNIS HOPPER, HOOSIERS, GENE HACKMAN

#32 FOREST WHITAKER, PANIC ROOM, JODIE FOSTER, CONTACT, JAMES WOODS, NIXON, POWERS BOOTHE

#33 LIKE A KID, MULTIPLIERS, SCHOLARSHIPS, A CAR POOL, TOMORROW, A YARDSTICK, A SHADOW

#34 JERRY LEWIS, MARK HAMILL, RICHARD GERE, GRACE JONES, HUGH GRANT

#35 JUDD HIRSCH, GLENN CLOSE, GEENA DAVIS, PAUL HOGAN, GOLDIE HAWN

#36 HELLO, AUTUMN, PACKAGE, SHOELACE, EXTENSIVE, SPELLBOUND, PORTERHOUSE

#37 JOINT, RUCKUS, STATION, CHLORINE, SUPERNOVA, RESTAURANT, HUMMINGBIRD

#38 HIS SIDEBURNS, A LIGHTHOUSE, THE INFANTRY, THE OCEAN, NIGHTMARES, IT WAS CANNED, A SAXOPHONE

#39 CITY SLICKERS, SUPERMAN, AMADEUS, THE THING, HIGH NOON, THE MATRIX, THE EXORCIST, KING KONG, 3, 4, 6, 2, 7, 1, 5, 8

#40 PIMPLE, ATOMIC, RAISIN, LOCKET, CHOSEN, TOILET, INTAKE, UNHOOK, DOCKET

#41 GERBIL, INSIDE, SPLICE, BOMBER, EXTEND, EXHUME, BACKER, MARKED, FRUGAL

#42 VOCAL, RABBIT, PEDDLE, SPANISH, FEARFUL, CUSTARD, CRUMPET, STAMMER, FOUNTAIN, DAUGHTER, 7, 8, 5, 10, 6, 4, 1, 9, 3, 2

#43 PANTHER, MUSKRAT, RACCOON, ANTELOPE, ELEPHANT, KANGAROO, CROCODILE, CHIPMUNK, MARMOSET, PORCUPINE, 4, 3, 6, 1, 2, 9, 10, 7, 8, 5

#44 EIGHT+TWO=TEN, TEN/FIVE=TWO, SIXxZERO=ZERO, SIX+SIX=TWELVE, SIXTYxZERO=ZERO, SEVEN+FOUR=ELEVEN, NINE+THREE=TWELVE, ONE+ELEVEN=TWELVE, FIFTEEN/THREE=FIVE, TENxTEN=ONE HUNDRED

#45 SEAN CONNERY, KATE WINSLET, MIKE MYERS, RENE RUSSO, ANNETTE BENING, KIM BASINGER, MORGAN FREEMAN, NICOLAS CAGE, 3, 4, 1, 6, 5, 8, 2, 7

#46 A ROBIN, A CHATTERBOX, NOODLE SOUP, DEVILED EGGS, GOULASH, HOMER, IN FINLAND

#47 THE MUPPET SHOW, ANOTHER WORLD, CHICAGO HOPE, COLUMBO, WAGON TRAIN, I LOVE LUCY, THE NANNY, THE OFFICE, 3, 4, 5, 1, 7, 2, 8, 6

#48 SWIVEL, SUNKEN, MUFFIN, SALOON, HANGAR, GUSHER, MARKET, SNEAKY, WICKET

#49 MASKED, NUDIST, CUTLET, GIRDER, PIGLET, SHRIMP, BRONCO, KILLER, EUREKA

#50 POODLES, RED TAPE, GRAVELY, A HOLE, A RIVER, A FEATHER, YOUR BREATH

#51 MERCY, FROLIC, CENSURE, DILIGENT, AVAILABLE, ESPECIALLY, INDEPENDENT

#52 PIANO, JOSTLE, MUFFLER, FATALITY, OBNOXIOUS, CONFERENCE, FINGERPRINT

#53 JOHNNY DEPP, LUCILLE BALL, KIRSTIE ALLEY, KEANU REEVES, JEFF GOLDBLUM, DEBRA WINGER, LIAM NEESON, GENE HACKMAN, 4, 2, 6, 7, 1, 5, 8, 3

#54 JOHN CUSACK, HIGH FIDELITY, TIM ROBBINS, BULL DURHAM, KEVIN COSTNER, TIN CUP, RENE RUSSO

#55 JON VOIGHT, COMING HOME, JANE FONDA, NINE TO FIVE, DOLLY PARTON, STEEL MAGNOLIAS, SALLY FIELD

#56 SANDRA BULLOCK, JIM CARREY, ASHLEY JUDD, BETTE MIDLER, VAL KILMER, MARK HAMILL, BILL MURRAY, HELEN HUNT, 3, 2, 6, 8, 1, 7, 5, 4

#57 REFUND, OCTANE, SHIFTY, SIESTA, THROWN, DRENCH, UNRULY, TWELVE, SAFETY

#58 FRUGAL, SLUDGE, TEACUP, RADIUS, ESKIMO, CHURCH, FOURTH, HACKER, HUMANE

#59 A NITWIT, A TUNA FISH, SCREENS, A BOTTLE, COLUMBUS, ZEBRA, SWORDFISH

#60 GROWING PAINS, BARNABY JONES, MATCH GAME, FANTASY ISLAND, PROVIDENCE, KNIGHT RIDER, MOONLIGHTING, NIGHT GALLERY, 4, 7, 1, 5, 8, 2, 3, 6

#61 FLEECE, VEGETABLES, A GLADIOLA, A SUNFISH, GROUND BEEF, I AM BUSHED, A CANNIBAL

#62 FINAL, FINISH, ROUTINE, KINDLING, MESSENGER, PHENOMENON, EMBARRASSED

#63 LOBBY, POLISH, ASHAMED, DIPLOMAT, DISPLEASE, MIRACULOUS, PESSIMISTIC

#64 STAR WARS, CHICAGO, HOME ALONE, ARMAGEDDON, TRUE GRIT, TOOTSIE, ALADDIN, NOTTING HILL, 3, 6, 2, 4, 7, 1, 8, 5

#65 LIGHTLY, DEAREST, APPOINT, FUNCTION, TRACTION, SEEDLESS, MARRIAGE, THROTTLE, CRACKPOT, REMEMBER, 2, 9, 10, 4, 3, 1, 8, 7, 5, 6

#66 EIGHTxONE=EIGHT, SIX+FIVE=ELEVEN, TWO-TWO=FOUR-FOUR, TWELVE/TWELVE=ONE, ONE+ONE=FIVE-THREE, ONE-TWO=NEGATIVE ONE, EIGHTY/FOUR=TWENTY, TEN+TEN=TWENTY+ZERO, THIRTY+THIRTY=SIXTY, TWOxFOUR=TWELVE-FOUR

#67 JEFF BRIDGES, SCOTT BAIO, RENE RUSSO, JOHNNY CASH, VANNA WHITE

#68 ALEX TREBEK, DICK CLARK, MEG RYAN, DIANE KEATON, MARTIN SHEEN

#69 POT ROAST, LIE STILL, A MINISTER, HOGWASH, WISECRACKS, POST OFFICE, IGNORANT

#70 FIGMENT, WEDLOCK, GRACIOUS, PHEASANT, GROUNDER, BASEMENT, SCRIBBLE, BANNISTER, GERMINATE, BLAMELESS, 9, 1, 5, 2, 3, 4, 7, 10, 8, 6

#71 LOU GRANT, ROSEANNE, THE WEST WING, PICKET FENCES, LOST IN SPACE, MIAMI VICE, BEWITCHED, MISTER ED, 2, 5, 7, 1, 4, 8, 6, 3

#72 BLOND, BALLOT, TEXTURE, KEEPSAKE, BEDSPREAD, METICULOUS, SHORTHANDED

#73 WOMAN, DIGEST, ACHIEVE, OBSTRUCT, COUNTDOWN, ACCOMPLISH, MERITORIOUS

#74 FUNNY, HORRID, ZEALOUS, CHRONIC, LOVABLE, BUOYANT, FORCEFUL, EFFICIENT OBNOXIOUS, WONDERFUL, 8, 7, 3, 2, 5, 6, 9, 4, 1, 10

#75 PARENTHOOD, A FEW GOOD MEN, AMERICAN BEAUTY, ANNIE HALL, PRETTY WOMAN, CAST AWAY, CHINATOWN, AIR FORCE ONE, 3, 1, 5, 2, 8, 7, 6, 4

#76 FIVE PLUS FIVE = TEN, TWO TIMES TWO = FOUR, ONE MINUS ONE =ZERO, TEN PLUS TEN = TWENTY, SIX PLUS THREE = NINE, SEVEN MINUS FIVE = TWO, TWO TIMES FOUR = EIGHT, FIVE PLUS SIX = ELEVEN, EIGHT MINUS EIGHT = ZERO, NINE PLUS SEVEN = SIXTEEN

#77 ROBERT DUVALL, PHENOMENON, JOHN TRAVOLTA, GET SHORTY, RENE RUSSO. OUTBREAK, KEVIN SPACEY

#78 KEVIN COSTNER, WATERWORLD, DENNIS HOPPER, BLUE VELVET, LAURA DERN, JURASSIC PARK, JEFF GOLDBLUM

#79 COURTNEY COX, AL PACINO, WINONA RYDER, RICHARD GERE, BRENDAN FRASER, ANGELINA JOLIE, BILL PULLMAN,HEATHER GRAHAM, 4, 3, 7, 1, 6, 2, 8, 5

#80 A WATCH DOG, FROSTBITE, CELL PHONES, A FENCE, ROOT CANAL, THEY CHARGE, TWISTER

#81 HONEY, THRIVE, ATTEMPT, FUMIGATE, INVENTORY, FLASHLIGHT, PREDICAMENT

#82 EMPTY, FACING, BIFOCAL, VELOCITY, NOSEBLEED, RETROSPECT, COMMUNICATE

#83 SUPERMAN, FULL HOUSE, THE COSBY SHOW, THE LOVE BOAT, BAYWATCH, GOOD TIMES, THE ODD COUPLE, JUST SHOOT ME, 5, 2, 7, 3, 8, 1, 4, 6

#84 FIVE/FIVE=ONE, EIGHT/FOUR=TWO, NINE+TWO=ELEVEN, FOUR+FOUR=EIGHT, FIVExFOUR=TWENTY, SIX+SIX=ONE DOZEN, SIX+SEVEN=THIRTEEN, ELEVEN+TWO=THIRTEEN, ONE HUNDRED/TEN=TEN, SIX+SIX=FIVE+SEVEN

#85 THE STING, GLADIATOR, RUNAWAY BRIDE, BASIC INSTINCT, PHILADELPHIA, MINORITY REPORT, CITY OF ANGELS, THUNDERBALL, 3, 5, 2, 7, 8, 1, 4, 6

ANSWERS

#86 SHARON STONE, BRUCE WILLIS, CLINT EASTWOOD, JACK NICHOLSON, JEREMY IRONS, MARGOT KIDDER, TERI GARR, JOHN MALKOVICH, 6, 1, 2, 4, 7, 3, 8, 5

#87 MEL GIBSON, LETHAL WEAPON, DANNY GLOVER, GRAND CANYON, KEVIN KLINE, WILD WILD WEST, WILL SMITH

#88 BRUCE WILLIS, PULP FICTION, JOHN TRAVOLTA, LUCKY NUMBERS, LISA KUDROW, ANALYZE THIS, BILLY CRYSTAL

#89 HOPSCOTCH, ICE SCREAMS, GRANDPAW, A BIG STINK, A WEBSITE, A FAUCET, YOUR PICTURE

#90 TRICK, RARELY, WEDDING, OVERRULE, AMUSEMENT, GOVERNMENT, NEGOTIATION

#91 GROUP, SENTRY, BARRIER, SWIMMING, ASSISTANT, ATTACHMENT, RATIONALIZE

#92 THE MASK, DEATH WISH, SYRIANA, THE GRADUATE, GROUNDHOG DAY, ERIN BROKOVICH, TOY STORY, MYSTIC RIVER, 3, 4, 6, 2, 7, 1, 8, 5

#93 FINCH, EAGLE, PUFFIN, PIGEON, CHICKEN, PEACOCK, SPARROW, CARDINAL, STARLING, BLUEBIRD, FLAMINGO, PHEASANT, PARTRIDGE, ALBATROSS

#94 FOUR PLUS TWO = SIX, ONE TIMES SIX = SIX, FIVE TIMES TWO = TEN, TWO TIMES TWO = FOUR, FOUR MINUS TWO = TWO, FIVE PLUS FIVE = TEN, SIX PLUS THREE = NINE, TWENTY MINUS TEN = TEN, TEN PLUS FIVE = FIFTEEN, ELEVEN MINUS TWO = NINE

#95 MATTHEW PERRY, JANE FONDA, HUGH GRANT, KURT RUSSELL, SALMA HAYEK, ANTHONY HOPKINS, RUSSELL CROWE, JODIE FOSTER, 4, 6, 2, 8, 1, 5, 3, 7

#96 A PICCOLO, YOUR LAP, A CABBAGE, A VOLLEYBALL, A BALD EAGLE, A PUDDLE, FAST FOOD

#97 DREW CAREY, ASHLEY JUDD, ANDY GARCIA, SALLY FIELD, HALLE BERRY

#98 PETER FALK, MERYL STREEP, CHEVY CHASE, PERRY COMO, MEL BROOKS

#99 BIG BROTHER, NEWHART, THE LONE RANGER, GREEN ACRES, THE FUGITIVE, BARNEY MILLER, THE MONKEES, PERRY MASON, 4, 5, 1, 6, 8, 2, 7, 3

#100 NEGATE, PICKLE, GOTTEN, BEACON, REVOLT, INVADE, GAZEBO, LOADED, DIVEST

#101 ISLAND, PLACID, GRAVEL, RESUME, NUTMEG, MUTANT, BIOPSY, MARKET, FRISKY

#102 CRACK IT UP, MILK SHAKES, YOUR AGE, I AM STUFFED, A SWALLOW, HE BUCKED, IMPORTANT

BONUS PUZZLES

ANSWERS

CROSSWORDS

#1

W	A	R	P		U	R	G	E		B	A	T	T	S
O	R	E	O		P	A	W	N		E	L	I	O	T
W	I	E	L	D	T	H	E	S	C	E	P	T	E	R
S	A	F	A	R	I		N	U	L	L		L	I	U
		N	A	G	S		R	A	I	M	E	N	T	
H	O	L	D	T	H	E	R	E	I	N	S			
A	H	A		S	T	L	O		M	E	E	K	E	R
L	I	M	B		L	A	S		C	A	G	E		
T	O	P	O	F	F		S	A	G	E		Y	O	N
			R	U	L	E	T	H	E	R	O	O	S	T
D	I	A	G	R	A	M		L	Y	N	N			
E	R	R		B	I	B	S		S	E	T	S	U	P
C	A	L	L	A	L	L	T	H	E	S	H	O	T	S
K	N	E	E	L		E	Y	E	R		A	L	E	S
S	I	S	A	L		M	E	N	S		T	E	S	T

#2

B	A	B	E		M	E	M	O	S		S	T	A	Y
U	R	A	L		A	D	D	U	P		K	A	N	E
F	I	L	L	I	N	G	S	T	A	T	I	O	N	S
F	E	Z		F	E	E		S	T	A	R			
S	L	A	I	N		I	O	C		R	U	M	B	A
		C	R	O	W	N	C	O	L	O	N	I	E	S
		A	T	E		T	R	O	T			C	A	P
O	M	A	N		A	L	O	E	S		M	E	T	S
R	A	G		D	R	O	P		E	G	O			
B	R	A	C	E	Y	O	U	R	S	E	L	F		
S	C	R	U	B		P	S	A		N	E	E	D	S
		R	U	S	H		N	P	R		D	O	T	
B	R	I	D	G	E	O	F	T	H	E	N	O	S	E
E	A	R	L		C	L	U	E	D		A	R	E	A
T	Y	K	E		T	E	N	D	S		B	A	S	K

#3

S	H	E	D		C	A	S	T	E	S		H	O	P
A	A	R	E		O	B	O	I	S	T		A	C	E
G	R	A	N	D	C	O	U	L	E	E		A	C	S
A	D	S		A	A	A			V	A	G	U	E	
	C	A	A	N		R	O	O	S	E	V	E	L	T
R	A	B	B	I		D	A	N	A		A	N	T	A
A	S	L	E	E	P		K	E	M	P				
W	H	E	E	L	E	R		B	O	U	L	D	E	R
			S	T	E	M		A	B	O	U	N	D	
S	L	A	W		E	N	O	S		L	I	L	T	S
M	O	S	S	Y	R	O	C	K		I	S	L	E	
O	U	I	J	A		I	N	S		A	R	M		
O	D	D		H	U	N	G	R	Y	H	O	R	S	E
T	E	E		O	P	I	A	T	E		A	D	I	N
H	R	S		O	N	P	O	S	T		S	S	N	S

#4

P	I	S	A		F	O	R	U	M		S	O	H	O
A	S	P	S		A	M	I	N	O		C	L	O	G
C	L	O	C	K	R	A	D	I	O		I	D	O	L
T	E	R	R	A		N	E	O	N		E	S	T	E
S	T	E	I	N	S			N	S	Y	N	C		
			B	E	I	G	E	S		A	C	H	E	D
B	A	S	E		T	A	X		C	R	E	O	L	E
A	L	L		C	U	S	T	A	R	D		O	L	A
R	E	A	D	U	P		O	W	E		A	L	A	R
E	X	P	E	L		S	L	E	E	P	Y			
		H	E	L	L	O		P	E	N	C	I	L	
T	R	A	P		O	R	A	L		G	R	E	T	A
Y	A	P	S		F	R	U	I	T	S	A	L	A	D
P	I	P	E		T	O	R	S	O		N	I	L	E
E	N	Y	A		S	W	A	P	S		D	A	Y	S

SUDOKU

#1

1	4	5	6	8	9	2	3	7
7	3	9	4	1	2	5	6	8
8	2	6	5	7	3	9	4	1
6	7	2	9	5	1	3	8	4
5	9	3	7	4	8	1	2	6
4	1	8	2	3	6	7	5	9
2	8	1	3	6	7	4	9	5
9	6	4	1	2	5	8	7	3
3	5	7	8	9	4	6	1	2

#2

7	3	6	5	4	8	2	9	1
8	1	2	9	6	3	4	7	5
9	4	5	7	2	1	8	6	3
2	9	1	6	3	7	5	8	4
5	8	3	4	1	9	6	2	7
6	7	4	2	8	5	3	1	9
1	6	7	3	5	2	9	4	8
4	5	8	1	9	6	7	3	2
3	2	9	8	7	4	1	5	6

(CONTINUED ON NEXT PAGE)

CHECK OUT PAT'S OFFICIAL GAME WEBSITE

PatSajak GAMES

www.PatSajakGames.com

BONUS PUZZLES

SUDOKU (CONTINUED)

#3

8	4	9	3	2	6	7	1	5
7	3	6	5	4	1	9	2	8
2	5	1	7	8	9	4	3	6
4	1	2	9	5	8	6	7	3
6	8	3	2	1	7	5	4	9
5	9	7	6	3	4	2	8	1
1	6	5	8	7	2	3	9	4
3	7	4	1	9	5	8	6	2
9	2	8	4	6	3	1	5	7

#4

7	3	8	4	9	2	5	6	1
6	2	1	8	5	7	3	4	9
4	9	5	6	3	1	7	2	8
1	5	2	9	4	3	6	8	7
8	4	9	2	7	6	1	3	5
3	6	7	1	8	5	2	9	4
5	8	3	7	6	4	9	1	2
2	7	4	3	1	9	8	5	6
9	1	6	5	2	8	4	7	3

#5

5	2	6	3	4	7	8	9	1
1	4	3	6	9	8	2	5	7
8	7	9	2	5	1	4	3	6
6	3	5	8	2	4	7	1	9
4	9	2	1	7	6	5	8	3
7	1	8	5	3	9	6	2	4
9	6	1	4	8	5	3	7	2
2	8	4	7	1	3	9	6	5
3	5	7	9	6	2	1	4	8

#6

1	2	5	9	7	6	4	3	8
6	4	3	8	5	2	7	9	1
9	8	7	1	4	3	5	2	6
3	1	6	7	9	4	2	8	5
8	7	9	5	2	1	3	6	4
4	5	2	6	3	8	9	1	7
2	6	4	3	1	7	8	5	9
7	9	1	2	8	5	6	4	3
5	3	8	4	6	9	1	7	2

TRIBOND

#1 BE BALD, BE DECORATED, HAVE HOODS, ANIMAL GROUPS, HAVE CHIPS, BE PRESSED, HAVE CABINETS, HAVE WHITES, TV HOUSEKEEPERS

#2 ON ISLANDS, HAVE NUMBERS, CHARLIE LINES, TYPES OF SHARKS, SMALLESTS, HAVE BUTTONS, BE LOADED, STATE CAPITALS, HAVE LONG NECKS

#3 HAVE RIMS, TYPES OF CRABS, MUSIC GROUPS, SHADES OF GREEN, HAVE RUNNERS, DELIVER, HAVE CORDS, HAVE CASES, PLAYED ANGELS

CROSSWORD CONNECTIONS

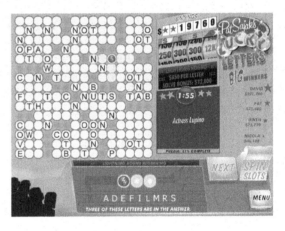 

ABOUT PAT SAJAK

Pat was born in Chicago, Illinois on October 26, 1946. He spent all of his young life in that city, attending both Goethe and Gary Elementary Schools, Farragut High School and Columbia College. He was the oldest of three brothers, and he remains so today, except even older.

His first chance to broadcast came in 1965 when his name was drawn on WLS Radio's "Dick Biondi Show" to be a "Guest Teen Deejay." Biondi was ill the night Pat was to appear, so he went on with Dick's replacement, Art Roberts, for a full hour that Saturday night, reading commercials, announcing records and trying to sound professional. He was hooked.

While attending Columbia College in Chicago (and working nights as a desk clerk at the Palmer House Hotel), one of Pat's broadcasting instructors, a local announcer named Al Parker (who passed away recently after an incredible 50-plus years at Columbia) told him that they might be looking for a newsman at a little local radio station called WEDC. Pat went in, read a few things for the Program Director, and was hired to work from midnight until 6 a.m. doing an hourly five-minute "rip and read" newscast (you ripped it off the newswires and read as it was).

In 1968, Pat left Columbia after only three years, joined the U.S. Army, and was promptly sent to Vietnam. After a few months as a finance clerk, he was transferred into Armed Forces Radio and given the morning show on AFVN in Saigon where he yelled, "Good Morning, Vietnam!" for a year and a half. He finished his military career at the Pentagon in 1970. After his discharge in late 1970, Pat stayed in Washington trying to find radio or TV work. With no success on the broadcasting front, he again found himself working as a desk clerk, this time at the Madison Hotel in downtown D.C. Finally, a friend told him that he knew someone who owned a radio station in Murray, Kentucky, and maybe he would hire Pat. So, in 1971, he became the nighttime disc jockey at a 250-watt station in southeastern Kentucky. It took about a year for this 25-year-old to look around and come to the conclusion that his career was not exactly "taking off." So he packed up his belongings and headed to the nearest big city, which happened to be Nashville, Tennessee. Despite interviewing at virtually every radio and television station in town, Pat found himself (again!) as a desk clerk at a local motel. He continued to visit the local broadcasting outlets and was finally hired by the local NBC television affiliate, WSM.

He spent five years at Channel 4 as everything from an anonymous staff announcer to a talk-show host, to a disc jockey at their sister radio station, but it was as a weatherman that Pat was getting the most on-air exposure

In Los Angeles, KNBC-TV was looking for a weatherman in 1977, and they spotted Pat in Nashville and hired him to be their full-time weatherman. He worked both the early and late newscasts, as well as a local weekend talk show called "The Sunday Show." One of those who sat home and watched was Merv Griffin. He called in 1981 and asked whether Pat would be interested in taking over for Chuck Woolery, who was leaving "Wheel of Fortune" a daytime game show on NBC, after seven years as host.

While Pat had done a few other game show pilots, most notably for Ralph Edwards and Mark Goodson, he never felt completely comfortable in the role. Assuming that "Wheel" probably had a year or two left in it, he agreed to step in. His assessment of its longevity proved to be off by a couple of decades. The nighttime version of the show went on the air in September 1983, and it has been the Number One program in syndicated television ever since.